BY MARTIN JOHNSON

SAFARI
LION

A LIBELED ELEPHANT.

It is a well-known legend that elephants are blind. I have not found them so. They do plod along as though half asleep much of the time; but this, I believe, is because they are so powerful, are secure from death at the claws of other beasts, and have grown careless with the centuries. When attacked by man they are as wide awake as anything that roams forest or jungle.

SAFARI

A SAGA OF THE AFRICAN BLUE

By

MARTIN JOHNSON

With 66 Illustrations

G. P. PUTNAM'S SONS
New York — London

SAFARI

∼

Copyright, 1928
by
Martin Johnson

Made in the United States of America

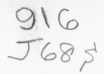

ACKNOWLEDGMENTS

The author wishes to express his appreciation to the following magazines for granting permission to include material previously published: *American Magazine, Collier's, Delineator, Good Housekeeping,* and *The Saturday Evening Post.*

All photographs reproduced in this book are by Martin Johnson and are copyrighted by the American Museum of Natural History.

CONTENTS

ILLUSTRATIONS

vii

ILLUSTRATIONS

FACING
PAGE

SAFARI

A SAGA OF THE AFRICAN BLUE

1

CHAPTER I

INTO THE BLUE

EIGHTEEN years ago I sold my small business and set out with Osa, my wife, to see the world. We sailed through the South Seas and explored the jungles of the Malay Peninsula. We now find our greatest happiness on the shores of our Lake Paradise home in British East Africa, hundreds of miles from civilization. Wild elephants and aboriginal natives are our nearest neighbors.

We are really not very different from other people despite the strange course our life has taken. We love thrills; and we love home. And we want to be pretty comfortable in both.

We have found Africa full of thrills. Wild elephants come right in and steal sweet potatoes out of our back yard up at the Lake. Silly ostriches dash madly across the trail when we are motoring. Rhinos tree us. Lions roar and hyenas cackle around our camps.

Yet never was there a home happier than ours. There is no corner grocery store. The nearest telephone is five hundred miles away. But we have

3

sunshine and laughter and flowers the year round. In a sense, we are King and Queen in our own right. At least we have that feeling up there in our little principality on the top of our mountain peak where lies our lake called Paradise.

There are no frills to our régime.   We dress to keep warm and eat to live. Simple pleasures stand out in their true values unsullied by the myriad artificial entertainments of civilization. Our diet is plain; our costume unadorned; we rise with the sun and labor while it lasts. As a result we find life more savory than ever it was amid the conveniences of hot hotels and traffic-jammed streets.

Mrs. Johnson and I sailed from New York on December 1, 1923. Our objective was to film, more completely than it had ever been done before, a record of Africa's fast vanishing wild life, in order that posterity might be able permanently to recall it as it had existed in its last and greatest stronghold.

From England we took a ship down around the Cape, and brought our huge cargo of equipment safely ashore at the port of Mombasa, on the East African coast a few weeks later. From Mombasa we took the little trunk line railway more than three hundred miles northwest to Nairobi, the capital of Kenya Colony and the last civilized settlement before reaching the wilderness. Our stay in Nairobi was a brief but busy period. It was there that we gathered our nearly two hundred porters and concentrated our mass of equipment. We had everything from sugar and pills to film, including big water tanks, hardware, flour, clothing, and a wide variety of other articles calculated to keep us independent for many months.

When we left for Lake Paradise, which is close to the Abyssinian border and nearly five hundred miles due north, we ran into the rainy season. Our six motor cars were loaded to their guards. We made a brave effort to elude the rain by going on a short cut up to the northeast. But the elements beat us to it. Less than half way along an incredible series of morasses as well as vicious rocky trails forced us to turn back and try the older and longer route to the north.

We left Nairobi at noon February 21st. On April 12th, at 3 o'clock in the afternoon, after innumerable hardships and adventures both with storms and wild beasts of every description we broke through the virgin forest and there was Lake Paradise right in front of us.

Osa was so happy that she cried.

Thick jungle closes it in. The lake lies in the crater of a dead volcano. At the moment of our arrival the sun glimmered on its blue surface. Thousands of birds twittered and called from the tree-tops around us as we rested from our toil. Down near the water were heron and egrets, while out on the surface floated ducks of half a dozen species, divers and coots. The trees were laden with moss. Flowers grew profusely everywhere. Best of all, right there at our feet, lay the fresh spoor of wild elephants.

Lake Paradise indeed!

Because others will want to follow in our footsteps it is only fair to give more of the details of our voyage out.

Someone who had influence with the steamship company arranged a very pleasant surprise for us. We had secured a good first class cabin on the steamer from New York but had not even got settled when the purser came and said that he had been instructed to give us a suite. So the first thing we knew we found ourselves in five palatial rooms with all our own baggage.

"I suppose we'll wake up any minute and find it isn't true!" laughed Osa.

Kalowatt, our Gibbon Ape, wandered from one room to another and was perfectly at home. She had been for long our constant companion, mentor and friend. We had run across her some years before in the interior of Borneo on a trip several hundred miles inland. On that occasion we travelled on a junk owned and captained by a Chinese widow, then by grass-roofed dugouts up the shallower streams of the jungle. Finally we reached a miserable little hut in a clearing in the jungle kept by a Eurasian and a Malay woman who looked even more dilapidated than their shanty. There on a chain, thin and spindling and half-starved, was Kalowatt, the cunningest little ball of fluff you ever saw in the world. Instantly my heart went out to her and so did Osa's. We bargained for her, at last agreeing on a stiff price, six dollars Malay or three United States. At parting, the poor woman whose ribs showed on her torso like bars and whose back ran in raw welts, wept bitterly; that much must be said for her. We hated to take Kalowatt away, but in the end she would only have starved. As it was, with proper care she soon filled out and was forever up to the most cunning tricks. She would eat at our table, using a tiny fork; would swing from tree to tree when we were on safari; or ride with us in our car or on one of the donkeys' or camels' backs. Whenever we stopped, she raced up the nearest tree with the most graceful agile movements, and hurried back again when she heard the motor's starting chug. And now, on our present trip to England, she found the steamer a fascinating new playground and kept us amused the whole way over.

We were met at Southampton by the manager of the Lens Company looking after our twenty-one cameras. I use American cameras entirely, both movie and still, but I make a specialty of having the best lenses money can buy. I still feel that no skin, head, book or other trophy of an explorer's journey can measure up in importance with an artistically made photograph. All my lenses are ground to order and each one thoroughly tested before I pack it.

Our reservations were in a small hotel that we usually patronize in London, and we were soon up to our necks in work, buying and packing the equipment that we still needed. I spent most of my time rushing about inspecting tents, beds, tables, water bottles, waterproof bags, and other equipment that was not available in Africa. I had found by experience that I needed bags that were really waterproof, beds larger than the usual little narrow cot, chairs that would not come to pieces in six months, and water bottles that would really hold water. And, above all, I wanted them made so that they would pack tight in loads of sixty pounds for our porters' packs.

In the end we had a total of over 250 cases and crates containing tents, beds, tarpaulins, chairs, tables, ground cloths, waterproof bags, canvas, fishing rods, cameras, acids, developers, guns, revolvers, rifles, and a thousand et ceteras it would take too long to mention.

It was strange, too, when one considers that we had come to Africa to study her wild life in a free and

LAKE PARADISE.

This picture was made from my mud laboratory window. In the evenings and all through the night the shores of the Lake were—and are still—a meeting place for the wild forest game coming down to drink.

TYPICAL COUNTRY SURROUNDING THE LAKE.

Vines and Spanish moss were sometimes so dense that we could scarcely get through. Old trees that had died many years ago were held upright by the tangled vines.

unmolested state, to go over the inventory of our arsenal.   We had:

3 English Blands—.470—double barrel
1 English Bland—.275—Mannlicher action
1 American Springfield—.303—Mauser action
1 English Rigby—.505—Mauser action
3 American Winchesters—.405—lever action
1 American Winchester—.32—lever action
2 English Jeffries—.404—Mauser action
1 American Winchester shotgun—.12—repeating
1 American Parker—.12—double barrel
1 American Ithaca—.20—double barrel
1 American Ithaca—.20—sawed off shotgun, called riot gun
1 .38 Colt revolver
1 .45 Colt revolver.

But emergencies might arise in which we should need them.

With everything boxed for shipment, gun licenses made out and all the other red tape fixed up, I spent two cold and miserable days at the Royal Albert docks getting my cargo aboard the S. S. *Mantola* of the British India Line.   I had to let money flow like water in order to get my things stowed away in safety.   My cameras and other delicate articles had to be carried carefully aboard and deposited in the baggage room where they would not be moved. My acids and movie film I had stowed in special moisture proof houses on deck. Incidentally, I caught a bad cold at the work; and the night before we sailed I topped my misery off by getting ptomaine poisoning from eating mussels in a London restaurant.

We left London in low spirits. The fog and our fatigue combined to depress us. As the *Mantola* had no heat I was glad that I had left out enough of my own blankets. Even when some days later we reached Port Sudan which I had always considered the hottest city on earth, we still wore our overcoats.

We dropped anchor at Aden for a few hours to take and deliver mail. At least half the native population came out with curios to sell.

On January 26, a midsummer's morning to be exact, we awoke in our berths to find ourselves no longer swaying with the midocean movements of the ship but lying almost stockstill. We glanced out of the porthole to find a harbor shimmering under waves of heat; big Arab dhows, high-pooped, open-waisted, vainly stretching their triangular brown sails for a capful of wind; a flotilla of row-boats all around us, their passengers halloaing to friends on our rail and eyeing the yellow quarantine flag, hoping that it would soon run down and so allow them on board.

This was Kilindini, the port of Mombasa whose white fort and government buildings and stores rose out of the heat waves, a mile to the west, on the other side of the island. To some these sights of British East Africa would have been strange. But we were as glad to see them as any homeward bound traveller when first the Statue of Liberty looms up over him out of the Upper Bay. Some 330 miles by queer wood-burning trains to the Northwest and we should be at Nairobi. And five hundred miles more due north would bring us to Lake Paradise, that green spot in a vast wilderness which now we called home.

If in the drowsiness induced by the heat and nine hours of slumber on Equatorial seas we had any doubt that we were nearing home, to reassure us there on a great flat-bottomed barge was Phishie, our old cook, come clear down from the Northern Frontier, with Mohammed, our watchman. Phishie was bravely rigged out in a new suit of khaki, in honor of the occasion; Mohammed still wore his *kanza* or native mother hubbard. At sight of us, both their happy faces shone like black melons suddenly split open to show rows of glistening white seeds.

It took us but a few seconds to dress, a minute to swallow coffee and be examined. Then the yellow flag ran down and I was in the waist anxiously watching the cranes lifting our freight down on the great barge which I had engaged by cable.

Our luggage once on board the barge, we made for the wharf, docked, and took a Ford for Mombasa.

There were two distinct streams of travel for the town, one made up of jitneys, the other of rickshas. Like the currents of different ages, they ran on side by side.

Mombasa is something of a metropolis, numbering about ten thousand souls, European white, Arab *café au lait*, swarthy half-caste, muddy-colored mongrel, and ink black. Once it resounded day and night to the whimpering of mothers torn from their children and the clanking of slave chains, for it was the great slave port of the Coast. Still can one see marks of conflict in the walls of its old white fort; and even now they often dig up skulls and rusted links buried in the sands.

But quaint as Mombasa is, we had no mind to linger there. After a good shore dinner and a night's sleep at a very modern hotel we left by train for Nairobi, to the northwest. The compartments of the train opened, English and Continental fashion, on the side. But what the original color of the furnishings were I could scarcely make out, for seats, floor, racks, were a dusty orange hue from the red clay country through which we passed. Even the usually inky faces of the porters had a lacquer of vermilion.

After a few hours we came out on the veldt, a scrubby plain, but still bearing signs of civilization at the stations which boasted restaurants not unlike

Fred Harvey's on our own Santa Fé. Also there were stands from which the natives sold cigarettes and fruit.

When we were awakened next morning by the red sun streaming in on our berth we found ourselves in a new belt. The cocoanut palms near the coast and the scrubby country through which we passed in the late afternoon had been left behind. All around us was a vast plain as far as the eye could reach, sentinelled by an occasional thorn bush or acacia and bulwarked in the distance by low-lying violet hills. At the stations the natives wore skins instead of khaki and mother hubbards, and carried shields and spears. Since daybreak we had been seeing wild animals.

What a joy it was, after six gruelling months in civilization, to see again the real Africa we had come so to love.

On either side of the track far to the distant hills, perhaps thirty miles away, the plain was covered with vast herds of game; horned and bearded wilde-beeste or gnus, ugly tusked wart-hogs, cunning little mongrel-like jackals, long-necked giraffe, gazelles, kongoni, ostriches, and striped clouds of zebra. Our queer beast of iron that ran on rails seemed to bother them not at all; indeed they scarcely looked up from their grazing as we roared past, for they had long since learned that a locomotive is not carnivorous.

We came a few hours later into the modern station of the town of Nairobi, our final stop before stepping out into the unknown. It is a place of about thirty thousand souls, nine-tenths black or brown. On the streets were splendidly appointed hotels; ladies beautifully coiffeured; natives clad in one-piece skins riding bicycles, others in G-strings; black traffic policemen with vertical rows of bone buttons and horizontal rows of teeth equally shiny; a beauty shop where Osa got her hair waved; several book stores; department stores; black girls in skin clothing gazing in the windows; tea parlors; huts of mud and grass, of hammered-out petrol tins; cars; humpbacked oxen; fine Tudor houses; the bar of the Norfolk hotel where hovered the ghosts of Paul Rainey, McMillan, Roosevelt; gardens of roses fenced in from the bush-buck; and a cemetery where only the week before a lion had killed a kongoni.

In Nairobi several friends met us: Blayney Percival, the retired game warden and crack shot, whose companionship and wide experience have been invaluable; Stanley of the Native Affairs office; Oscar Thomson, the acting American consul; and Bob Gil-fillan. We had a fine luncheon with them at the Norfolk, the rendezvous of so many mighty big game hunters.

Of course we had our luggage to attend to and in the afternoon, after lunching with a group of old friends, I returned to the station, to find the black porters wildly flinging my cases on the motor lorries. Since these contained the highest priced cameras and camera materials I had ever owned, one may imagine my feelings. Sometimes I think these boys are thoroughly unreliable. Though they are big and husky, they are so muscle-bound I can outlift and outrun any of them. Again I like them. At any rate, on this occasion, with a little well applied persuasion, they were soon working carefully and cheerfully, all singing away as if nothing had happened.

This singing of theirs, or rather chanting, is always helpful as a stimulant to toil. I cannot transcribe it in musical terms. There seem to be no formal songs nor verses handed down from generation to generation. The men sing, no matter at what task they are engaged, handling luggage, thatching grass huts, sharpening spears, skinning game. Even on safari, they often break into song, unless too hungry or tired. Each accompaniment suits the particular task in words, tempo and rhythm of the tune. They always stress particularly the note that accompanies the heave or lift; and when any task is done they wind up with a sibilant *psssstt!* If you have ever seen sailors working at the winch you can imagine the effect. I'd call it a sort of negro Volga Boat Song or African sea chantey.

Through the early weeks of February we were busy unpacking our cases, making up the contents into packages of the right sizes for porters and camels to carry. We were also buying things which we had not needed to ship down and which were used on safari, such as hardware of all sorts, galvanized water tanks, khaki clothing, sugar, coffee, and the native *posho*. There were also our splendid Willys-Knight motor cars to uncrate and assemble, and hunting licences to get, in case we ever found it absolutely necessary to shoot. In Africa these are rather expensive. One takes out a general license to shoot all the common game, the allowance being definite for each kind, though lions, zebra, leopards and hyena are unlimited. Special licenses are issued for elephant, rhino, giraffe and ostrich. We took out all of these, for though we should never slaughter recklessly, there might come times when we had to shoot straight and true to protect our lives.

All these weeks I was choosing my native boys, porters, gun-bearers, house servants, cooks, and headmen. While all lived in native districts near Nairobi, their blood was that of a score of widely scattered African tribes. Many of them had worked for us before and the news of our arrival had been spread far and wide by some mysterious underground telegraphy. I did not have to worry therefore about hands, but I did worry about oxen and wagons,

ORYX AT A WATERHOLE.

Up in the reeds a couple of hundred yards away there is good clear water, but all game dislikes going into bush or reeds to drink, as such cover may harbor lions. So the animals drink this muddy alkaline water in the waterholes. Oryx often fight among each other, and often we saw them with only one horn, which made them look like Unicorns. Perhaps they are the animal which gave rise to the original Unicorn legend.

HIGH NOON ON THE SERENGETI PLAINS.

Note the wildebeeste gathered around the trees. They are optimists for there is not enough shade for a dozen animals, let alone the hundred that sometimes crowd around. For fifty square miles around the plains are dotted with game just as represented in this picture—probably millions of head.

for there was a gold rush on down in Tanganyika and every available ox and transport had been gobbled up.

However, by sending messages and runners to the Boer farmers roundabout I managed to secure a few oxen, and Percival, whose sure hand and experience were to be with us for a time at Lake Paradise, got me over a bunch of thirty mules from a Nairobi cartage concern. Later I had a total of sixteen oxen besides my mules. My wagons and lorries, heavily loaded, I now sent on ahead, northward to Isiolo, two hundred and fifty miles on the way to Lake Paradise, the latter being our home and the greatest game sanctuary I have ever seen. I had already sent word to Isiolo to two friends, Dr. McDonough and Rattray, the former being government veterinary and the latter busy catching and training zebra. I asked them to put up my transports and look after my boys until I arrived. I then wired to Nyeri, a hundred miles north, where there was a lonely telegraph station, and ordered four more ox wagons with a hundred loads of *posho* and four hundred gallons of petrol, as well as lubricating oil and kerosene, to proceed to the rendezvous at Isiolo. I was relieved when I got word that all were on the way. The rainy season was due in about a month. If it should strike us sooner my transports would

become mired and all my photographic materials
might be ruined.

Altogether I had about as much trouble with my
transportation problems as a general of the A. E. F.,
and now there was the problem of recruits. The
most experienced and capable I selected out of that
black host of grinning faces that had already mobilized from all over East Africa.

To start, I enrolled Ndundu, a wise and crafty
gun-bearer, good at his job, but temperamental and
as vain as a turkey cock when given a little authority;
Japandi, a skinner, who had been with the elder
Roosevelt; Omara, a Meru, whom we would use as
gardener at Lake Paradise; Abdulla, a Buganda, for
chauffeur and mechanic; Jagongua, a big strapping
Kavarando, for head porter of cameras; Thu, a young
Kikuyu, to help with the simplest work in pictures;
Nasero, a Minumewasa, as assistant head porter
and gun-bearer, for he fell just short of the ability to
have charge of any important job; Suku, a young
Meru, as first boy or body servant; Semona, a
Buganda, for second boy; two Merus whose names
I cannot remember, for rough carpentering; and
above all, Bukhari, my head man, a six foot Nubian, black as ink, powerful of limb, statuesque of
feature, and a real African aristocrat.

There were others, of course, who would serve as
ordinary porters for carrying things on safari, cutting

down trees, smoothing rough spots in the road, and blazing trails through the jungles; but with those mentioned by name we had closer personal contact.

As a farewell to Nairobi we gave a picture show at the Royal Theatre. It was a great sight, peeping out from a point of vantage near the screen, to see in the native section of the theatre some of my old hands sitting motionless except when they gave way to chuckles of pleasure as they saw themselves pictured on a safari during our first African expedition.

The next morning we packed a few extras in our passenger cars. Among these were twenty pounds of butter in salt, four dozen eggs in sawdust, a boiled ham, twelve loaves of bread, and safari biscuit for use when the bread gave out. Also there were cameras, tripods, tarpaulins and tents, and such things as we needed on the ride up to Isiolo, where now our main caravan was encamped. Then we set out, coasted over a splendid modern road kept in shape by native labor, through plains with only an occasional head of game, and put up that night at Thika, at the Blue Posts Hotel. This hostelry consisted of sixteen straw-thatched sugar-loaf huts, each hut being a numbered room. We fell asleep quite happily to the music of two waterfalls a few yards from our hut.

CHAPTER II

OUR RACE TO PARADISE

MY heart sank when I saw how slow our progress north was and realized at the same time that the rains were only two weeks off. We simply had to get across the Guaso Nyiro river before it was in flood or the season would be lost. The rains, I knew, would make such heavy going that it would be impossible for our motor cars to get through by any other route.

One great comfort lay in my fine Willys-Knight cars which I had brought along for what proved to be certainly the toughest work to which any motor cars in the world have ever been put. It is a pleasure at this writing to say that my confidence was not misplaced.

Six cars went on ahead of us all piled high with our stuff until their tormented springs cried out for relief. As I was afraid of the tsetse fly country through which we must pass I soon got rid of my last mules and took only oxen.

We left Nairobi serious enough at heart. It was not so much the danger that worried us, though that would threaten us often enough when the time came. We could shoot and had learned through many years of exploration how to handle ourselves in the wilds. But we had grave responsibilities; heavier burdens, sometimes I thought, than any we put on the backs of our camels and donkeys or the black boys who chanted so gayly as they safaried on "into the blue." Then there were the human souls, the natives, who had entrusted themselves to my care. They could trail elephants and lions, of course, but many would die by the way because of perils I ordered them to take. They were well paid for it; but none the less it would be my fault. And there would be fevers, illnesses, wounds ahead; we had no physician or surgeon with us, and I must undertake those rôles as well as that of commander of this little army. And if I was concerned for them, I was much more anxious about Osa. Despite her years with me in the field, she was bound to be lonely at times. Her love of adventure, of fishing and shooting, her joy in wild animal life, would carry her a long way; but how about the times—and they would come—when she longed for friends, for new clothes, theatres, dances, all those things which can never wholly satisfy any worth while woman but which every worth while woman craves once in a while. And suppose she got ill, with no other white woman within call.

As for the objective of our expedition, it was all a

gamble. The accomplishment of our main purpose was by no means so sure no matter how perfect our equipment nor how high our hopes. We had come twelve thousand miles, and were spending a fortune to take pictures, make a real screen story of African wild animal life, free and unmolested—all without directors, sets, and the trick and captured animals which are common to the usual commercial film.

I do not often worry, just do my best, and let fate take its course; but I did think of these hazards as we listened to the tinkling of the waterfalls that first night on the trail. And in the morning, when I awoke, Osa was not by my side.

I had, however, no sooner thrown on my clothes than she came bursting in, with a string of fat catfish which she had caught by the waterfall.

At breakfast where we had a bottle of beer apiece, as a last toast to Civilization, and three each of Osa's sweet-fleshed fish, we made up. Osa found a weighing machine in the hut that served as office for the hotel and weighed herself and me, finding that we had already lost several pounds. That is always the way. In New York we get stout and soft, eat too much rich food; I smoke too much and after a week or two we are both thoroughly discontented. But out here "in the blue"—a name that comes I suppose from the blues and violets of the ever vanishing horizon—we quickly harden, lose flesh, and can endure any hardship; and, except once in a while when our expedition seems threatened with failure, we sleep like tops.

After weighing in, we drove on, I leading, Osa at the second wheel, Abdullah at the third, through the plains country, rising a little now as we came into the Mount Kenya district. From then on we came into the real country, the Africa we love. We were now about six thousand feet above sea level and game began to appear in droves. Hitherto we had seen only occasional prowlers; but here hartebeeste the common striped zebra, and the dainty Grant's gazelle, galloped over the high plains. Flocks of ostrich, black-plumed cocks and brown females, fed quietly until we came abreast. Then they would start running parallel with us until we put on more power, when, as if challenged, they would spurt and gain—we simply could not keep up with them—until they were a hundred rods ahead. Satisfied then that they could beat us, they would leave the softer ground by the road, turn, and cross in front of us, often awkwardly sprawling in the rockier road bed. If they went through this programme once, they went through it fifty times. Osa and I laughed until we cried; for lovely as they were in flight, they were absurdly grotesque when they doubled on us.

We were going through magnificent country all these last days of the trip up to Isiolo. Sometimes the roads were so smooth that we tried to go in high gear, but found we had to climb in low; the ascent was so gradual that it was deceptive. For mile after mile we wound up and down rocky trails within a few inches of the edge, looking down on little swiftly coursing streams, up at tiers of green-wooded ledges and a maze of trembling white scarves of waterfalls. All around us the latter plunged and smoked and bubbled from the green walls, as if designed by some master scenic artist.

Often when the road curved round the shoulder of some hill or when we looked down a red vista of cliffs, we could see, sometimes at fifty, sometimes at seventy miles distance, Mount Kenya—green at the foot and to three quarters of the way up, then red, violet and blue in the craggy belt near the top, and snowy white at the peak. Like an image of winter in the arms of summer, she stood exactly on the Equator; and we should have liked to have visited her. For there, we knew, were all manner of beautiful birds and beasts, the most luxurious of flowers; and we had once picked flowers that looked like violets upspringing there by the elephants' trails. But as we could not delay, with our caravan eating off its head at Isiolo, we had to be content with the sight of those noble snowy peaks dominating the plain wherever we went.

Late that night, after crossing several ice-cold

OSA TROUT FISHING IN A TYPICAL POOL.

This is one of the streams at the foot of Mt. Kenya that are filled with rainbow and brown trout. The trees overhead shelter beautiful Colobus monkeys, and the whole surrounding countryside abounds in game, both great and small.

No Trouble at All.

Rainbow trout Osa caught at Nanyuki where the cold streams from Mt. Kenya make an angler's paradise. One of these trout weighs five and three quarters pounds, and the other, three and a half.

streams fed from the snows of far-off Kenya, we came on a faint trail. As we went we stirred up bustards, quail, sand grouse, and the ugly vulturines, which flew disturbingly about us like shadows of the dusk, sometimes darting over the windshield into our faces. With the dusk we reached a hill below which twinkles the flickering lights of a little native settlement. Vaguely we made out the huts of the quarantine station, saw flocks of zebra behind a manyetta or native corral and heard our men busy around their fires.

Anxious as we were to reach our destination, Lake Paradise, we could not leave the present neighborhood until we had secured more oxen and camels and wagons; so we had a week to spend with Rattray and McDonough. However time did not hang heavy on our hands. Beyond Isiolo, stretching north of the river, was a great plains country with high grass on a red clay soil sanded white. This we explored standing sometimes on giant anthills twenty feet in height. From these queer eminences we could see thousands of head of game—all kinds of gazelle and the greater antelope, oryx, and retic- ulated giraffe ambling along with necks bending forward in their queer fashion. All around us, too, swarmed game birds, bustards with their big fluffed heads, grey brown guniea fowl, as well as grouse, and spur fowl. Here and there grotesque vultures with long necks and an undertaker's look swooped above their quarry, or sat in grim circles around a dying zebra, waiting for him to die and sometimes hastening on his end by climbing on his panting striped withers and pecking at his glazing eyes.

Osa bagged some game birds and spent much time at fishing in the Isiolo. The stream was so covered with green vegetation floating on its surface that often when I came towards her, it seemed as if she were pulling the carp-like silver fish right out of the grass.

Where we roamed either on the plains, or in the scrub country south of the river, we saw great droves of native goats and cattle. It was sort of a general *hegira*, for the different tribesmen were bringing down their herds from the frontier for trading in the south. McDonough, as head of the quarantine station, had his hands full; the cattle here are afflicted quite as they are in the Argentine or Texas; those on one side of the river being subject to hoof and mouth disease, those on the other, to fever.

Rattray's place itself was fascinating. With his manyettas or corrals of upright palings, his bomas or barricades of thorn-bush, tame oryxes running around loose, spur fowl breeding with Plymouth Rocks in his dooryard, and tamed zebras learning to trot in double or single harness, his ranch looked like a zoo.

Though we didn't see him tackle any more leopards bare-handed, as he had once before, we had proof of what his powerful hands could do when we followed him up to one of his bomas or game corrals and saw him grab a full grown gerenuk that had drifted in during the night. The gerenuk is a gazelle with a neck so long that it reminds one of a cross between a gazelle and a giraffe and is now found only in this part of British East Africa. This one was a young buck with horns, and was standing in its peculiar fashion on its hindlegs with its forefeet against a tree browsing on the twigs or tender buds of the branches.

Two Meru boys who were with us watched the bout between man and animal with astonished eyes. On their return they described it all over the many-etta. Now Rattray is more of a hero than ever. It is one thing to shoot wild animals with guns or spears and poisoned arrows and quite another to tackle them with bare hands. They think he is the bravest and strongest man in Africa; they are not so far out of the way, either.

After all we were glad to rest here a few days to await Percival, so that we might explore the desert north of the river for good trails to Lake Paradise, for we had so far taken a route new to us from Isiolo up. I had the boys build a few huts by the river on the edge of the stream. With their knives they cut down trees, others dug holes, and a third band gathered and bound sheaves of grass for thatching. The temporary shelters were soon completed.

Osa's share of the work consisted in furnishing game and fish. It was strange, her passion for this sport, for she comes from an inland and rather dry country; but all of her ancestors were quick with the rod and rifle. And she came in so smiling and happy with her glistening fish—one night she had a twenty-five pound catfish—that I could not forbid her to go on her expeditions, though she sometimes strayed pretty far from camp and often forgot to take her gunbearer. Of course, she can shoot and I'd rather have her by my side than most men in a pinch, but now on the plains at night we had already begun to hear the roar of lions and leopards.

One of the most damaging encounters I have ever had with wild animals in Africa came at this time. I carelessly leaned against a tree down near the river and dislodged a hornet's nest. Its angry inhabitants promptly made for me, and in a minute I was stung in a dozen places and one got down my back underneath my shirt. At the end of an hour one eye was closed and the other swollen nearly so; my upper lip was puffed out big as a goose egg; and I had bumps all over my neck and the top of my head. My back felt like one solid boil. I developed fever and altogether had a bad night of it. Worst of all was the fact that all the sympathy I got from my wife and my comrades was a lot of hearty laughter.

Percival joined us at the Guaso Nyiro river on March 6th. He had left Nairobi a week after us in a rattle-trap old Ford car. His vehicle was so patched together with rope and wire that I wondered what made it go. He brought a native driver to take it back, a wild-looking Wakamba with filed teeth. Percival was pretty well done in when he reached us, having travelled night and day with his car limping most of the way. He had used his last drop of gasoline crossing the river. Had we camped any further on he would have had trouble finding us.

Time was flying and the rains getting closer and closer to ruination of my plans. On March 7 I took one of the cars and three boys and drove north to look over the possibility of getting through the mountains ahead of us. It was necessary to find out if the trails would be passable for our ox wagons and lorries. When we reached Lake Paradise we could safari out after game in trackless deserts on camels. But now we had to use these machines which were utterly out of character in the desert drama to convey our things to the mountains and beyond. Besides, they do make better time, infinitely better, though they destroy the atmosphere. However there was atmosphere enough, with the great desert stretching for miles to the north, a red

clay base sanded like a barroom floor, with little sad
bunches of grass here and there, a mournful-looking
and lonely thorn tree perhaps and only an occasional
little mound which reminded me of the old theatrical
seas a generation ago, with their great sheets of
fabric to get an ocean effect while boys' heads bobbed
up and down underneath to make the waves. Well,
there on the Kaisoot Desert, it seemed as if only an
occasional boy were on the job, so rare were the
waves. The vast expanse was like a grey sea asleep.

Now and then, too, as I rode, I would see on this
moth-eaten mangy desert a hyena, like a hideous
yellow dog with his fore-legs longer than the rear,
making him walk as if his back were broken.
Occasionally, as I neared the infrequent waterholes,
I would startle a herd of zebra, which would kick
up their heels and then gallop away only a little
more real than ghosts because of their black stripes
and buckskin. When nearing the Ndoto mountains,
once up a donga (a rough craggy red gully like our
Montana coulees) I startled a lion over a zebra which
lay on its side, its belly swelling and its legs out
straight in the rigor of death. Nearby lurked little
doglike jackals. The natives say that the jackal is
in cahoots with the lion; that the jackal is his scout
or little black bellhop and tells him of easy kills.
Then when he has performed his task well, the lion
allows him his commission or tips in nice zebra or

giraffe meat.   They have many quaint explanations, these blacks, but this one seems almost sound. Anyway, there were the two jackals dining away peacefully side by side with the king of beasts on this striped filet.

After three days of reconnoitering I returned to camp and found Percival with a story similar to mine.   He had followed a second trail on foot, striking the mountains at a closer point than I did.   But there was no sign of a way through for our heavy vehicles.   We held a council of war and sadly agreed that it would be a waste of time to try any further along this route.

I passed a miserable night.   Hour after hour I lay awake thinking of the hardships we had undergone to get this far, the money it had cost, and the strain on man and equipment; and now we had to turn back and do it all over again in another direction.   And, I knew, there was every chance we would succumb to the terrific rains long before we reached our goal.

Before daylight I had reached a decision.   I knew our boys would start grumbling the minute we turned back.   So before breakfast I had the porters lined up, *posho* rationed to each one for four days and started them all back to Archer's Post.   They muttered in their own tongue; but with full bellies they took it pretty well, all things considered.

After a hasty breakfast I struck out for Isiolo, making the fifty miles in four hours, fair racing speed for this wild country. At Isiolo I found that Rattray had left for Nairobi. I rushed on to Archer's Post fifteen miles away and left orders with Mohammed Sudan, the black clerk in charge, to have my porters, when they came in, return for another load as quickly as they could. Then I put on full speed back to camp.

Now it began to rain. I left Archer's Post at 9 P.M. in a downpour which soon made muck of the going. At 10 I nearly ran into a group of a dozen hyena, who were dazed by my light. At least fifty jackals ran ahead of me at different times. About midnight four fine maned lions and a lioness ran across my trail and into the bush. A little further on two lion cubs were playing in the road. Their mother, a fine-limbed lioness, jumped out, defiantly faced me a second, then the three slipped off into the darkness. At a place called "Kipsing" by the natives, I encountered three rhinos rooting in the sand. They faced me and snorted angrily at my intrusion, then trotted off. I killed many birds that flew into the light and were blinded. As I had no windshield several hit me in the face.

It was a nightmare, that ride; and one that will stay in my memory. I arrived back in camp at 3 P.M. all in, and too utterly exhausted even to sleep.

A MEMBER OF THE FAMILY.

We sleep in our cars while on safari. Naturally Kalowatt, our Borneo Gibbon's
Ape, who traveled with us for nine years, makes herself at home.

KALOWATT SICK IN BED.

Kalowatt was intensely human, and in this instance her expression showed
plainly how sorry she felt for herself.

Two Uses for Automobiles in Africa.

Above—Crossing the northern Guaso Nyiro River on the Northern Frontier, where we often had to wait a week for the water to go down.

Below—Osa's new Wyllis-Knight in Tanganyika. She always drove it herself, and sometimes we were able to go hundreds of miles across the wide plains.

For five days we relayed our stuff back to Archer's Post. Osa was a brick. Few women could have stood the hundred miles a day of struggle with the spirit and courage she did. We were both worn out when it was over.

Now my boys began to get ill. I sent back several Meru who were in a bad way. A few more deserted.

March 29th found us plugging northward again, now across the Kaisoot desert on a more familiar trail to Lake Paradise, one which we had worked out for ourselves on our first visit some years before. When our cars stuck, it was a case of dig and swear, load and unload, haul and push, from dawn until midnight. One night millions of grasshoppers invaded us. Next morning we found the camp black with the remains of those which we had trampled down.

On April 2 we struggled into Kampi ya Tempr, the government boma or station. Here we found Lieutenant Harrison, a young Englishman with twenty-five Askaris who had been stationed in this god-forsaken spot for seven months. The place consisted mostly of a few mud huts and a little cattle.

'While we were having lunch a black fellow came up and saluted, addressing Osa and myself by name. He turned out to be an old friend of a former expedition, a native named Boculy, whom I had been trying to trace ever since we had landed. We called the fellow "half-brother to the elephants" because of his uncanny knowledge of the beasts. He could find them where no one else would dream of looking and was about the only black I have ever known who could really track an elephant successfully. The lieutenant was kind enough to say he would loan him to us; at which Boculy grinned all over and darted off to gather up his blankets.

We spent a day in camp rubbing our sore limbs with Sloan's liniment and tightening our loads for the next test. On April 5th we moved camp ahead to where we turned off from native trails towards Lake Paradise. Now we were going up more rapidly and the country began to get more wooded.

It was on April 12th that we had our first meeting with the elephants. Boculy suddenly paused in the trail ahead and waved his hand. Watching him stealthily, we could almost see his lips form the word "Tembo," Swahili for elephant. Right ahead was a fine young bull with forty pound tusks, calmly pulling the branches of the trees down so that he might graze on the tender shoots. Sleepily he munched his fodder. It made me sick at heart not to have my camera. He was perfectly posed and in a beautiful spot for pictures. Even the light was perfect. The wind being right, he did not get our scent but went on eating as if there were no white man within a thousand miles.

Then suddenly he heard some sound or, the wind veered and he caught our scent; for he stopped grazing and melted into the forest.   It is a trick that elephants have, most astonishing when one considers their huge bulk, the way they vanish so noiselessly into the green.

There were thirty-six more hours of blazing a trail by pounding rocks and felling trees, and then we reached a little open space on what seemed to be the top of the world.   All around the clearing was the emerald of wood and vine; beyond, as far as the eye could reach, the great desert, for all its reddish grey waste a magnificent sight because of its vastness. Then, two hundred feet below us, in a hollow of an extinct crater, girdled by forest aisles, shimmered with a thousand shades of blue and green that cup of sweet water which we call Lake Paradise.

CHAPTER III

WE DIG IN

IT took us several months to get built and organized at Lake Paradise because in effect we were establishing a permanent colony where Osa and I expected to spend most of our lives thenceforward.

Of course there was strong temptation to start right in on our work of hunting and exploration. But we didn't succumb. There were many weeks of work ahead before our rough camp could become a permanent base.

Osa and I were determined to be comfortable. Our theory was—and still is—that the best work in the field is done when one is in the best of health and good spirits. Nothing means more to health than cleanliness of food and person, and the surroundings in which both are enjoyed.

Promptly our small army of half-naked blacks got busy under the direction of their leaders and set about building our village. We could have gotten along with a small lodge for ourselves and lean-tos for the natives. But our plan was to have a real residence, mess shack, laboratory, store-houses, drying houses for ourselves; and good family cottages with rain-proof thatched roofs for the good men whom we had selected from the natives to be our retainers.

To give a clear idea of our base it is first necessary to give some sort of picture of the lake beside which we had settled. Imagine, if you will, first a gradual slope starting twenty miles south of here, swelling up to this three-peaked mountain, volcanic but now extinct. So long has it been extinct—for ages, just how many, no one can guess—that the earlier reds, violets and blues of its slag and subsoil are covered now with every imaginable shade of green, save in the patches of cliff not yet concealed by the clambering vines, and around which innumerable animals for innumerable years have worn hard trails.

A lake—our lake—a mile long and a half-mile wide, fills the summit of the age-old crater. Its edges are covered with vegetation, not stagnant and motionless, but ever swaying and floating and shimmering with a thousand shades bordering on blue and green. On it float coots and ducks; on the limbs of trees overreaching the water sit wise old storks; in the marshes wade blue heron and flamingo with their sunset breasts.

Opposite where we camped rose sheer cliffs seemingly impassable. Nevertheless, with the glass one could pick out trails around them and circling the borders of the lake; all worn down and baked hard from centuries of travel, not by men, but by generations of elephant, buffalo, and rhino.

Then, all around the lake, stretched miles of forest aisles of splendid African timber. The trees were festooned with pendant mosses and alive with voices, the trumpeting and crashing of elephants, whine of hyenas, gossip of baboons. The very passes, too, were filled with wild flowers after the rainy season, masses of blossoms where elephants trod, scarlet ones like pompoms around which butterflies flitted. And for fonts in this natural cathedral there were little waterholes and many waterfalls whose lacy veils were as fine and white as a bride's.

Place all this, then, on the roof of the world overlooking the great desert, as if you lived in a tower never before dwelt in or assaulted by man; then reflect on the fact that game came here to drink when Cleopatra sailed up the Nile, even when Noah stood by his ark's sail and laughed with his sons, one of whom fathered these black men that range forlornly with their cattle far below; and you can guess at part of the thrill we felt and something perhaps of the inspiration.

Percival had an interesting theory about how the water came into Lake Paradise and I think he was correct. He brought the subject up one night as we sat smoking.

"It is a curious lake," he observed. "Have you any idea how it is fed?"

"That is easy," I replied. "Rains are caught in the crater which forms its bowl."

"No, that theory won't hold. There is too little slope on the crater to catch much water; what is caught would evaporate quickly; and by the end of the dry season you'd find your lake gone."

"Springs, then," suggested Osa.

"Wrong again," Percival replied. "This is the highest point for hundreds of miles and you wouldn't get all that water from underground springs. What I believe is that it is fed from other lakes at higher levels way up in Abyssinia that discharge their water through underground rivers which find their way here."

"You told me," he added, "that when you were here before you noticed a net loss by watermarks of three feet each year. If we could find this other lake, you'd find that it too was lowering at the same rate; and perhaps your great-great-grandchildren will find no lake here at all or else only a rhino wallow."

We couldn't, however, imagine any such fate for this beautiful body of water, probably first visited by an old missionary two hundred years ago who wrote that old yellowing book, which had originally aroused our curiosity and led to the lake's latest discovery. No, we simply would not believe that the lake would ever disappear, especially as it was now so full and its square mile of area shimmered so beautifully before us in the moonlight.

Anyway all our theories were put to flight by Osa's stage whisper: "Look there!"

She pointed down to a little park-like space of about five acres, fairly clear, with a few great trees on it. These trees were all rubbed smooth on one side by animals scratching their backs and flanks. Indeed, one may find the same characteristic on all the trees by the trails of the forest. Some are smooth on one side up to a distance of fifty feet, showing that generations of game have there rubbed their sides, and the growth of the trees has carried the smooth marks upwards.

To this five-acre clearing a great trail led from the forest, and down it a rhino and his mate were coming. As they approached the edge, the disturbed waterfowl rose from the surface of the lake and whirled and circled in the moonlight.

After drinking with great gulps, which we could clearly hear, the beasts began to graze and approach our shore, their great bulks almost black against the moonlight gold, and the two horns on their snouts clearly silhouetted and looking for all the world like quotation marks. As the wind was just right they did not catch our scent. Besides, since we were above them they did not see the flames of our fire.

A Typical Night Scene at Lake Paradise, not Very Far from Our Front Door.

Rhinoceros, leopards, and buffalo pass up and down the trail to the waterhole all night long. Often we would go down to the waterhole at sundown to study them. We learned that, as with human beings, each animal has its personality and soon we came to know the different members of the same family. The young rhinoceros is usually tied for a long time to its mother's apron strings and is afraid to leave her even when almost full-grown. Here the mother is in the foreground.

A Flash that Boomeranged.

When I made this flashlight at Lesamis waterhole on the Kaisoot Desert, I forgot to shut my eyes, so both myself and the rhino were blinded. It was a toss-up as to which of us was the most frightened.

Finally they came so close to the shore under us that we could have pitched pebbles on their backs. Then suddenly they either caught our scent or smelt the fire, for they made a charge up the trail leading towards us and we began to shift in our chairs. The three black shapes in those chairs must have puzzled them, for they stopped midway in their charge and turned back, disappearing without causing us further concern.

To the reader's natural query as to how we kept our peace of mind at nights with so many wild animals around I can say that we made it routine for the boys to bring in dry wood at the end of each day for our night fires against our wild neighbors.

Osa was responsible for starting this routine. During one of our first nights, when we were still in tents, a rhino came right alongside the one in which Osa and I were asleep. Probably he got very close before he saw the white ghostly mass in the darkness. He snorted loudly, whirled, pawed up the ground, ran away a short distance; whirled again and snorted and then ran off into the forest. Osa was frankly scared stiff, and I didn't blame her. She dislikes rhino more than any other animal, and she said she had been dreaming about one of them when she was awakened by the first snort. She gave me a good scolding for letting the fire go out. Then she took the law temporarily into her own hands to call Bukhari from his own tent and give him orders to have a man keep the fires up all night from then on. And that was that.

Because of the unending rain we hurried the building of permanent quarters as much as possible. Most of the construction of shacks in British East Africa outside of Mombasa and Nairobi we had found rather crude. Prevailing style, if you care to call it that, was mud and straw thatch or, nearer the railroad and highways, hammered out petrol tins. Usually the frames were made of tree poles hastily cut with knives instead of axes, and tied together with twine made from vines, the whole covered with a dubious plastering of mud and thatched with bunches of grass.

We wanted something much more durable. So we made our poles thicker and sank them deeper in the ground; constructed stout sets of laths tied with jungle twine, poured pebbles and mud into all the spaces between, then stuccoed the whole with buffalo, elephant and rhino dung. We took extra precautions by mixing the dung with clay which made a serviceable exterior and interior wall. Previously all the dung had been pressed by the boys who gathered it, packed in pits, mixed with water, then trodden down hard much as peasants press grapes in the French provinces. When weathered a little the color, like that of Chinese punk which also is made of dung, was not unattractive against the green background when topped by the yellow of the thatched roof.

With this thatching too we took extra pains. On our dwellings we had a double roof to make an air space and secure greater coolness in summer.

On the interior walls we applied a shellac of paint and glue, and papered the whole with Marduff, or rough calico sheeting, which sometimes serves in British East Africa as currency. This done, Osa took the wooden cases which contained my photograph materials and which were of fine smooth boards and made good flooring for our living quarters.

We were not without comforts. Our living room was fourteen by seventeen, had a fireplace, a kitchen and bathroom in back—we had brought along a tub— and there was a porch in front. We also had a house for sleeping quarters; a store house, a laboratory building, a dark room, and a dwelling for such guests as might take it into their heads to come on from America, though there seemed little chance of that. Around the garden, like a row of barracks, were the porters' and native boys' huts, of the usual crude construction which they seem to prefer. As their stuccoing with handsful of mud hastily thrown on did not stand much weather I could foresee much time lost in repairs every time we had a storm. However, it is useless to try to train the natives in the white man's ways in so far as their own living is concerned.

In these first weeks we were very busy. Despite
the incessant rain the camp and forest presented a
very lively appearance which must have astonished
the hyenas and jackals that prowled about as well as
the innumerable colonies of baboons assembled in the
trees. We were always up with the sun. After
breakfast one gang would go off to get clay; another
to fell logs with their knives; others would gather
dung, treading it in the pits, or gather vines for twine
and tie bunches of grass for thatching. Within the
manyetta, or inclosure, house boys would be digging
postholes or rearing frames, working with the vegetables, and milking the cows. Silent but industrious
were Abdulla as he worked over the cars, and the
Meru carpenters, whom I simply could not teach to
lay logs in Western cabin fashion. They always
insisted on placing them upright, as their forefathers
had done since the time of the flood.

Osa too was very active. She attacked the store-
house, which was to hold our posho corn meal; put
hinges on the box covers; made shelves of jungle
grass; and planted flowers and vines around our living and sleeping quarters. But the busiest of all,
I think, was Kalowatt. She would swing from tree
to tree with her graceful gestures, then suddenly
pounce down on a black boy, seize the arctic wool
cap which the native insists on wearing even on
the Equator, then run up on a limb or ridgepole

and survey her angry victim with mischievous satisfaction.

Of course, there were days when all things did not go smoothly; when the boys were too tired to chant as they sang; and we had many malingerers. The first week we had none, the second week three; by the fifth eighteen reported at my laboratory for the evening clinic. However, I fixed them. To the very few that really seemed sick I gave a reasonable dose of quinine or whatever the patient seemed to need; but to the malingerers I gave a whopping big table-spoonful of powdered quinine and four tablespoonsful of castor oil to wash that down. Then I made each squat down for a quarter of an hour and stood over him to see that he did not spit up the dose. The next day my clinic had only three visitors.

There were times, too, when Percival and I had to make our rounds and rout out the boys who in the middle of the morning lay sleeping in the jungle despite the cobras and leopards which lurked about. A few well-directed kicks, however, soon set them at work and on the whole we had comparatively little labor trouble.

And still it rained. I have seen the play "Rain" in New York and have been to Panga Panga several times but never have I seen it rain as it did here. It seemed as if that one first moment of sunshine when we reached the summit and looked out over the lake was the only one to be vouchsafed us to show us what the country could be like. Nevertheless, we kept busily at work, some gangs going up the back trails to help the delayed transports, while others started building our shelters. And though, even when it stopped raining, the trees still dripped cold moisture on us, I kept the boys cheerful by rationing out extra lots of sugar and coffee and slaughtering oxen for fresh meat, a pleasing variation from their regular corn meal or posho; and we managed to keep great fires going somehow, part of the time, so that they could dry themselves before going to sleep.

In the early stages our boys were most miserable of all, having not even our insecure shelter. When the foremost wagons arrived and we put up our first tents, Osa called the boys and made them come under the tent porch flap where they squatted, grinning as Osa called out from within little jokes as old as Ham of whom we have just spoken, such as "It's a good day for ducks," nevertheless new to them. Her cheerfulness under all sorts of hardships was part of the secret of her charm, also of her power over them.

It was like Osa to start a garden in spite of the rain. Scarcely had we started unpacking than she had a big bundle of garden seeds out, checking over its contents. On the second afternoon she mustered a gang of boys with shovels and picks and cheerily started them digging a garden in the mud. The spot she selected was on a well-drained hillside and not quite as hopelessly muddy as on level ground. Percival and I only jeered, saying the seeds would rot if the birds didn't eat them. But we couldn't discourage her.

Her courage was rewarded in due time by a crop that still makes my mouth water. She had beans, peas, sweet corn, carrots, potatoes, cucumbers, turnips, squash, salsify, cantelope and watermelons. She was proud to the bursting point of her achievement; and I confess Percival and I had to take a back seat in agricultural matters from then on. Many days she wandered about amid her fruit and vegetables, weeding and picking bugs, rain or shine. Luckily she was able to get more boys to help her at this time because our work was constantly delayed by the torrents that streamed from the heavens upon our unprotected heads.

During all these weeks of hard labor, we fared very well at meals. Phishie and his boy gave us regular English breakfasts of bloater or kippered herring. Often we had ham and eggs, for Osa's original seventeen chickens soon increased to fifty, then to a hundred, then to two hundred. At luncheon and dinner we had all the vegetables in season—peas, beans, cucumbers, sweet corn and melons, which she had so carefully tended; and Phishie delighted in making my favorite floating island pudding and in serving *hors d'œuvres* on special occasions. His pleasure came in tempting our appetites, not in the dishes themselves; for when he had cleared away the most sumptuous meal, he would squat down on his haunches and reverting to type, eat his ground posho and water with only an occasional bit of oxen steak. Omara, his helper refused even this, saying that God had made the oxen, as well as everything that breathed, brothers to man; therefore it was wrong to kill and eat them.

Even when our larders later became depleted, we had delicacies from the wild. Osa would go out and come in with armsful of asparagus from the forest. Here, too, she found a delectable wild spinach, wild plums, rather bitter raw but delicious as jam; a black cranberry, very sweet and good; a native coffee, with great beans; a fruit resembling apricots with seeds like those of apples—a favorite with elephants; and trees oozing with brown honey.

It was, in short, a Robinson Crusoe life; or, since we were so many, an existence like that of the Swiss Family Robinson; with modern adaptations, of course, in our cars, machine shops, developing tanks, and wiring. Otherwise we were primitive enough. And the settlement, when finished after many moons of labor, was picturesque with its collection of over-hanging yellow thatches; the laboratory as the thirty-

A CORNER OF LAKE PARADISE.

The Kaisoot desert stretches away in the distance. At the right can be seen the roofs of our houses, and in the center, the main trail to the Lake. For centuries elephants have made their way nightly down this trail to water.

OUR FIRST HOME AT LAKE PARADISE.

The mud and dung and grass home we lived in before we built a better home of logs a few hundred yards distant. Elephants actually pulled off the grass from the roof while we were asleep inside. Note Lake Paradise in the distance.

foot skyscraper; acres of climbing beans and tall corn spears; our little army of blacks; the mobilized motor lorries, cars, and ox wagons; flocks of chicken and spurfowl; herds of donkeys, humpbacked cows, and camels; and Kalowatt, an army in herself—all set within that thirteen-foot stockade of palings and thorn bush on an eminence above the green lake in the heart of great forests which grew on the roof of the world.

Sometimes it seemed to us like an African adaptation of a Western trading post.

I was overjoyed when I set up the electric light plant and the engines started off with the first turn of the wheel. Luckily I got the battery liquid just right on the first test and the batteries themselves were in first class condition, despite their rough journey up to the Lake. As a result I had lights in my laboratory in no time. I had not planned to use electricity in the other houses, although I know the natives would have gotten a big kick out of such a luxury.

It may sound funny to be talking about a bathroom out there in one of the most inaccessible camps in the African wilds. But religiously night and morning I had our personal boys bring clear sparkling water and fill our tubs.

On the floors of all our living quarters we spread the skins of wild animals, although it must be remembered that our own expedition was not for hunting except in a pictorial sense. When we killed a lion or elephant it was solely to save our lives and not to boast that we had broken a record. We never fired a shot except when absolutely forced to do so.

One stove was finished the very first day. It was built on the order of a separate fireplace, with large boulders especially selected for their size and color. We had one head cook and several kitchen assistants. Everything that we used in the way of pots and pans was kept in a state of the most scrupulous cleanliness.

Strange to say, Osa's narrowest escape from injury in Africa came not from a wild animal but from cooking. We were cooking a juicy young guinea fowl. It was cleaned with its feathers on. Then Osa wrapped a damp towel around it, placed it in a hole in the ground with a little sand and a lot of hot ashes. The whole thing was finally covered with a thick layer of more sand to keep the heat in.

After about two hours she knew the bird was done. At her word the black cook opened the hole. Suddenly there was a loud explosion and a fragment of red hot stone whizzed past her head, striking one of the porters on his cheek and causing a deep cut and burn. Had Osa not moved a moment before she might have been killed.

I later found this is not an uncommon occurrence. Stones often explode in this region when heated.

Most of them are of fairly recent volcanic origin. Gases have been sealed up in them for centuries. So when they are heated the gases expand and burst them open. Natives say there are many accidents of this sort.

Osa was delighted when I installed our laundry. I had a special building erected where all our washing was done in big tubs by the natives. Clean boiling water was used and real irons and ironing boards. All this paraphernalia fascinated our African help who possessed no clothes to launder.

With the completion of our settlement, the rainy season stopped. It had not rained all the time, of course. After the first four or five days of heavy downpour, the heavens usually contented themselves with a good shower between middle afternoon and sundown, and there were strips in the desert below us which had very little water during the two and a half months of this season. But we were glad of the advent of fair weather for now we could set about making the pictures for which we had come over so many lands and seas.

Our final housewarming we celebrated by a great barbecue of oxen which I had bought from the neighboring Boran wanderers, and by the wild chanting of the hundred odd natives in camp.

CHAPTER IV

"LITTLE HALF-BROTHER OF THE ELEPHANTS"

A WORD about our boys and their cousins up country whom we came so well to know. I think our most difficult problem was to understand the workings of the native mind. For instance, we soon found that when washing clothes our boys would use a cake of soap per garment if we let them. They loved to see the bubbles—and they believed that cloth could not be cleansed except by rubbing the soap directly on it for a long time. Once we got a shipment of soap flakes. These were a total loss to the natives because the flakes disappeared before they could be rubbed in for any time at all.

Of course they couldn't read signs on our food tins. I remember one day I left a can of cleaning compound on the kitchen shelf. The dining room boy thought it was salt and placed it in our salt tin. Osa baked bread with it and the dining room boy filled the salt cellars with it. The cook flavored the soup with some more of it. You can imagine the excitement when dinner time came and everything had a rank alkaline taste. It was some time before we could solve the mystery.

We had some trouble with our fuel, which was wood and very smoky. But Phishie, the head cook, an inky black Swahili, finally became a past master of keeping red hot coals under the stove top without more than the faintest wisp of white vapor rising through the chimney.

One day Phishie came over to where Osa was putting some bulbs into her flower garden. He is over six feet tall and usually very graceful in every movement of his lithe body. This morning he was behaving awkwardly, hitching from one foot to the other and grinning foolishly. Osa thought he was going to apologize because she had just jumped all over him when his last batch of bread was not quite as good as it should have been.

"What do you want, Phishie?" she asked him when she saw that he couldn't quite get up his nerve to speak.

He grinned a six-inch grin. "I want to tell you, Memsab, that I think her man some day be as big as fine elephant," he said.

For the fraction of a second, Osa thought the boy was trying to be fresh. But that is the last thing in the world he would have done, I know. So she nodded seriously and said, "Why do you say that, Phishie?"

"Because Memsab is such a good cook," he responded.

Apparently, he was trying to pay Osa a compliment and congratulate Martin all in one stroke, to say nothing of getting back into her good graces after the calling-down he had just received over the bread.

The natives were by no means as particular about their food as we. Of course we made sure that they had plenty to eat. That is one of the secrets of keeping a safari crew happy and industrious. At the same time, we had to watch the men to see that they did not gorge themselves just before some especially hard job was to be undertaken.

My messages, which I had sent out from Nairobi by native runners all over the North, had borne good fruit. Scores of black boys and men had appeared out of nowhere, at our rendezvous at the quarantine station. I was particularly glad to see a tough-looking wise old Swahili who grinned and hailed me as "Bwana Piccer" (Master Picture), a name the natives gave me because of my calling. Two years ago he had been one of my porters and had been charged while on duty by a rhino. His stomach had been as badly ripped open as the horses in the Spanish arena. At the time I thought he would die, and left him with an Indian dresser at Meru where for months he lay flat on his back. But here he was, a little changed from his original pattern, but otherwise quite hale and hearty.

Among the others that came in were two promising looking huskies with heads smeared with red clay, wearing anklets of colobus monkey, and carrying fine spears with ostrich balls on the ends. At once they elected themselves headmen, refused to recognize the authority of Bukhari, my chosen headman, and tried to usurp his place. As they held some sort of influence over the other blacks, I had to humor them until my caravan got under way; but I determined to fix them when once I had them out in the desert.

My force of blacks now numbered seventy, all seasoned men, though not as yet very well disciplined. For vehicles, I had my group of Willys-Knights, several ox wagons, veritable droves of Abyssinian donkeys—not so well disciplined, either—and a lot of ungainly camels. With these, every man and beast heavily laden, we made an imposing caravan on the trail.

One morning our safari was changed into a hell when we saw clouds of dust on the horizon and an army of Samburu came loping up, with vast herds of cattle, camels, goats, and donkeys. You never heard such a bellowing and bleating, nor smelt such a stench of sweat, black flesh, stale one-piece skins, and dirty cattle. Worst of all were the swarms of flies which, like a plague of Kansas seventeen-year locusts, settled on our windshields, swarmed over our food, covered every inch of our faces and actually made the groves as dark as night.

Down to the river brim the Samburu women drove their donkeys, laden with gourds for water, where they filled these natural urns, meanwhile screaming at and tongue-lashing each other, while their ferocious-looking helpmates stood around us, many files deep and bristling with spear-heads.

At first the encounter seemed very ominous. A stranger to the desert would have been apprehensive for his life. But impressive as was that bristling ring, we knew we had little to fear. The black seldom attacks a white man. In Africa it just isn't done. Every tribe seems to take for granted Caucasian superiority. Indeed, so thoroughly is it recognized that the native is just a little scornful when the white man fails in anything he tries to do, though none of the miracles his master performs seem to impress him. I have taken boys from the frontier down to the station and waited for the reaction when they saw their first locomotive. They never gave it a second look. Perhaps this was because they had seen my motor cars and electrical equipment and were so impressed by our witchcraft that after that anything was possible for *Bwana*. Not being interested in machinery for its own sake, the locomotive

CARAVAN OF DROMEDARIES.

Contrary to general belief and the advertisements, these are *not* camels. The camel has *two* humps, the dromedary, one. Among the unexplored waterholes of the Ndoto Mountains we took our best elephant pictures. Here it was necessary to use large herds of camels. When we safaried from our home at Lake Paradise we sent the camels ahead to the appointed camp and followed in our cars, covering in two hours the distance which took the camels three days. It always gave me a peculiar feeling, as if I were turning Time backward, to park the cars and go off into the unknown with these ancient carriers.

MAKING CAMP IN THE ELEPHANT COUNTRY.

It takes about thirty minutes for a well regulated safari to make camp. Some boys go after water—others put up tents—the cook starts dinner—each has his work, and no time is lost. Here the dromedaries are being off-loaded on the edge of the Kaisoot Desert.

was just another iron horse.   But once let me have
engine trouble on the desert and fail to fix the car
instantly, and I fall in their esteem.

They do not seem to envy us any product of our
civilization.   I have already told how Phishie, our
cook, can serve cocktails and *hors d'œuvres* and make
a delicious floating island pudding which the boys
serve perfectly; but when the meal is over, the three
squat on their haunches, eating their *posho* from
rough bowls, though they could have anything we
have ourselves.   Suka, our house boy, sometimes
wears a suit of khaki; but when he visits his father,
who is clad in a G-string and plowing his fields with a
sharpened stick, he flings off that khaki and goes
ninety-nine per cent naked around the manyetta.
None can be more hysterical than he at a native cere-
monial or dance.   Except for wages sometimes, fresh
meat or a cigarette, the white man has nothing that
the black man desires.

So we were not at all concerned by these armed
warriors that had descended like wolves upon us;
especially as a minute after their arrival they discovered the little mirror at the side of one of our cars.
They were black statues no longer.   Immediately
there was such a shoving and pushing as no one ever
saw at a subway rush or a Donnybrook fair.

Among their herds were some camels whose looks I
liked; and after each warrior had surveyed himself in

the little mirror to his heart's content, I started to bargain for them. The process was worse than the purchase of a rug in a Cairo bazaar. There is a standard price prevailing in East Africa of a hundred shillings; but for formality's sake they asked two hundred and stayed pat at this price from dawn to dawn. It seemed almost as if they enjoyed seeing me swat their flies. With sunup, however, they agreed on the terms which they knew from the beginning of negotiations they would in the end have to accept. Then they drove off, leaving us the five camels and every one of the flies.

On the trail in the Mt. Kenya district, we passed hundreds of Kikuyus clad in one-piece skins and G-strings, and surrounded by thousands of bleating goats, on the trek for new grazing grounds. They seemed to travel very slowly, moving on for a little piece, then stopping while their herds nibbled the short bunch grass which formed a scant cover in this dry season for the red clay ground. During these pauses the herdsmen squatted on their haunches by the trail. Such a jabbering and blahing of herdsmen and goats you never heard!

Once in awhile Osa would signal me to stop and she would converse with them in Swahili, at which she had become more expert than I. This is a sort of African Esperanto understood by the native tribes which roam Tanganyika, British East

Africa, and even Abyssinia far to the North. Like
Yiddish, which is a conglomeration or polyglot of
Hebrew, Bohemian, German, Slavic and Spanish, it
is made up of native dialects and Arabian terms,
first stirred into a lingual goulash by the old Arab
slave traders who used to range these parts, driving
their chained gangs of blacks before them down
to Mombasa where they were shipped to all parts
of the world. The purest Swahili is spoken around
Zanzibar and has its grammar, newspaper, magazines
and more permanent literature. The tribes like
these Kikuyus which we met by the trail used a sort
of bastard or cockney Swahili; but it could be easily
understood by any white who had been for some time
in the country and who was at all observing and
attentive.

To this dialect or African Yiddish are daily being
added new terms, due to the advent of Europeans.
For instance, we have now *statione, post-officey*—they
seem to like this Italian-like suffix—for station and
post office. And we had no sooner started our
engines again than Abdullah called out to Osa that
there was something the matter with her "motor-
car's foot." She had a flat.

These Kikuyus and their herds, and the little
dukas, or native stores, sugar-loaf in shape, thatched
with straw, or made out of hammered-out petrol tins
and offering for sale penny's worths of sugar and

cheap coffee and cigarettes, were the only signs of life we saw in their neighborhood. At the *dukas*, little black boys would come out and stand there, stark naked, at salute—a trick they had learned from the King's African Rifles, the National Guard of blacks, officered by whites, which patrols this region.

We had learned to handle natives on our previous visit and during our years in the South Sea Islands; to like them also. Boculy was our best guide— the "Little Half-Brother of the Elephants." I think he knew the pachyderm family better than any man living. He could tell their size and speed and the direction of their travel by a crushed leaf or a broken branch. A mere handful of tracks would reveal to him the number in a herd.

We were fortunate indeed in employing Boculy. He was born on the slopes of Kilimanjaro, but he seems to know every mountain and river, in fact, every waterhole in Southern Abyssinia and British East Africa. Somewhere in the wilds he has a thousand cattle and two hundred and fifty camels, which the Borans or some one of his wandering tribe tend for him while he is on safari with the white man. The languages of each of these plains and desert people he knows and he surpasses the chiefs by far in intelligence. By a sort of free masonry he can secure aid from them when we need it; and a mere look from him or a wave of his hand will drive away whole tribes from waterholes when we want to take possession and make pictures.

Altogether he is Napoleon and Mussolini rolled in one, though he seems to have no organized following. He is contented with the exercise of his power only for some immediate necessity.

In endurance, too, none equal him. He will slip away like a ghost of the desert on some mysterious errand, fade away "in the blue," trek hundreds of miles without tent or blanket or food and water-bottle, traversing wastes where we know from experience the waterholes are fifty to sixty miles apart— then reappear, his mission accomplished, and take his place in camp quite as if he had left us but the minute before.

But it was not the mystery of him nor the inscrutability of his wise old face that most impressed us. It was his baffling knowledge of all the four-footed inhabitants of the wild and their ways, particularly of the elephants to which he is little half-brother.

He seemed to have a peculiar and almost supernatural instinct for game. He could scent it like a bloodhound. One morning, as was his custom, he had been up at sunrise and off to a waterhole three miles away, where, he assured us, we would find plenty of "*tembo*," or elephant. How he knew they were there was beyond us, since all the elephants had migrated from the forests with the big rains. But it was always safe to trust Boculy.

He did not speak but waved us on, leading the way with his peculiar crablike shambling gait up more dongas and through the brush. Every now and then he would stop like a pointer dog, bend down, pick up a piece of mud, examine it, and shake his head in affirmative or negative. If the evidence of the trail seemed to be satisfactory, he would examine the earth for a few yards roundabout, then pick up the trail again.

What he saw we could not see. Sometimes, so he afterwards explained it to me, the mud dropped from a hoof would tell part of the tale, for rhino, elephants, and buffalo choose different kinds of mud for their baths. Sometimes he could tell that particles of mud had come out of the crevices between the toes of *tembo;* again the bending of blades of grass, crushed leaves, and so on, would betray not only the kind of game but the direction it had taken and its goal.

Further, the condition of the bruised blades of grass to him was eloquent. It takes only three hours for trodden grass to spring up again; he could tell the time of passage by the angle. Finally, knowing the locale and the beasts' habits and rate of speed, he would predict the very spot where we would find the herd.

Such signs as these were difficult for us to read; but there were other and far more obvious ones. The spoor, for instance, varied with the kind of game; and its condition too would reveal the time of passage; while in wet ground or soil easily impressed, one could find three-toed rhino or hippo prints, which are the same in size but different in outline. I got so I could even distinguish between these and the tracks of elephants; for the elephant has four toes and as he lifts his foot always scuffs a little. Some say sex too can also be detected, alleging that the female elephant's print is oval, her mate's circular.

White hunters have learned to read these more legible tracks; but, unlike Boculy, they are easily fooled. Often we would have trailed a herd because there were lots of hoof prints when our guide would not have given it a thought. He had observed the abundance of small tracks of the totos or baby elephants, evidence enough to him that there would be no ivory—bull elephants usually keeping by themselves during the nursing season. "No *pembe* (ivory)," he would say.

The woods overhead were another open book to him. He would pick up a dislocated branch and tell you within five minutes of the time a herd of something or other had passed that way. Or he would look up at the trees and notice that the tender buds had been eaten off clean while the branch was

unbarked and unbruised, showing that big "*twigga*"
(giraffe) had lately grazed there. A hundred yards
on, he would call "*tembo*" where branches had been
pulled down, disjointed, and bark stripped by the
clumsy elephant who does not graze daintily as does
the giraffe but goes lumbering along, his trunk carelessly rifling the trees and leaving an unmistakeable
trail.

I kept up with him in the field as often as I could,
for his lore to me was fascinating. When I asked
him more about tracks, he pointed out the different
prints—those of the buffalo, whose sharp hoofs cut in
where no elephant's hoof makes a mark and which
utterly kill the grass that the elephant only bruises;
the leopard, whose pad differs from the doglike
cheetah (the former's claws being sheathed when he
walks) and also from the hyena, which leaves a mark
like a four-leaved clover with the petals all on top
while the leopard's is shaped like a water lilly.

As for Simba, King of Beasts, Boculy explained
he does not leave many marks. His prints, if you
ever find them, are round like the leopard's but much
larger; and the easiest way to track him is to find his
kill. As he usually drags this into the bush for
uninterrupted enjoyment you will not find him far
away. His padded course leaves little disturbance of
the ground. And the only marks on vegetation are
the wisps of hair on the thorns which, I am sure,

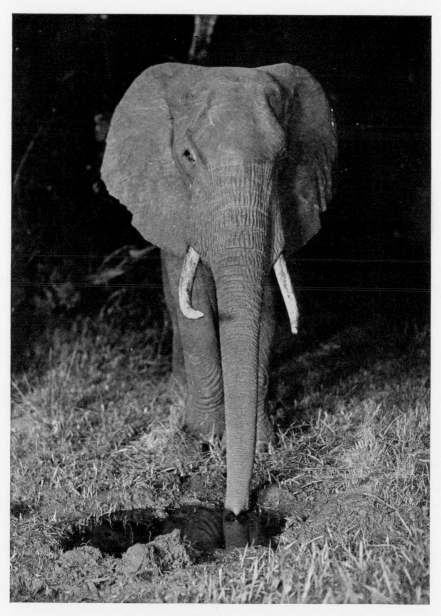

A HERMIT VISITS THE WATERHOLE.

This female must have been very lonesome, for during the three years we lived at the lake we saw her quite often and she was always alone. In this instance she has come down to have a solitary drink at the home-made waterhole where we got other elephant and buffalo pictures. Sometimes two pictures were taken at the same time, by cameras about twenty feet apart.

BOCULY, THE GREATEST OF ALL ELEPHANT TRACKERS.

Boculy's powers are uncanny. Born among elephants, and having spent his life in their native haunts, he can foresee their slightest move better than any man in Africa. Every blade of grass, every footprint so faint that no one else can see it, tells him a thrilling story.

prevent the growth of those fine manes one sometimes sees in captivity.

Much of Boculy's skill, I thought on reflection,
could be cultivated by the white man if he gave years
of time and concentration; but never the finer points.

Boculy was an exception even among the Africans.
None of our other hunters, skinners or gunbearers
even remotely approached him. I know I was in
despair when on the plains he would look four miles
away and pick out, from what I thought just a violet
rose-red blue of crag and sand and bush, a motionless
rhino which, even after being posted, I could hardly
discern through the binoculars.

But we did not appreciate Boculy's craft at first
and sometimes as he shambled along, seemingly half
asleep like his half-brothers, the elephants, and muttering to himself, I thought he was just fooling us,
pretending to examine the earth in which we could
see no marks of any kind, and going through the
motions to earn his *baksheesh*.

"He's a faker," I said to Osa, one day. But she
had more confidence in him.

"Give him a chance," she replied. "He looks to
me as if he knew his business."

She had no sooner said this than Boculy stooped
in the grass; posed motionless like a pointer again;
picked up more bits of mud; looked at some leaves;
sniffed the trail this way and that on all sides for

about a rod; then said,—"Bwana, over by the Old
Lady Waterhole (a name Osa had given one of the
small oases), you will find five bull *tembo*, four
females, and three little toto."

It was unbelievable, but when we climbed some
more boulders, cut down a flower-strewn ravine and
came to a great grove of mimosas watered by a
cascade falling into a natural saucer our faith was
restored. There quietly grazing were the elephants
our black paragon had promised us.

That even Boculy was human I discovered one
day when he called me aside, saying he had something very secret to tell me. He then proceeded to
confide in me that we should never get pictures so
long as Ndundu, one of our other guides, was with us.
It seemed, he went on to explain, that Ndundu had a
peculiar kind of blood which caused all the game to
leave as soon as he came into a neighborhood. The
manner of the animals' leaving was for them to vanish
into thin air. Before he confessed all of this to me
he had convinced my other porters of its truth.
However, so rotten had our luck been just then that
I was almost ready to believe it myself. It took a
lot of tactful talk to dispel Boculy's dark beliefs.

One day I asked my laboratory boy why he didn't
take a bath, once, say, in six months. In the warmth
of the little room in which we worked I found his body
smell particularly offensive.

"God made water for hippo, not for black man," he explained smilingly.

"But you smell," I told him frankly.

He turned on me a serious liquid brown pair of eyes.

"Bwana," he said, quite without any intended rudeness, "to the black man you smell too and very bad. Even the elephant not like your smell as much as black man's."

Again I gave it up.

The easy-going ways of the natives in the many-ettas, or villages, which stretched at great intervals throughout the plains, were quite as incomprehensible. Some of those whose homes I had visited would take it into their heads to come three days on safari just to say "hello." Perhaps they thought I might present them with something or have some work they could do, but if I didn't, and merely gave them a curt "hello," they wouldn't feel at all unhappy about it. Time meant simply nothing to them.

When they were given work, they were often unreliable. In sending them on errands I had to insist on their bringing back something as proof that they had reached their goal. Sometimes it was a bullet from Boculy who had gone ahead; again the merest trifle, useless, but which I pretended I wanted so that they would not fail.

Often I thought they didn't know what the word gratitude meant. At least what one did for them

did not seem to arouse that sense. The white man
was superior; it was his place to look out for the
weak, though often he robbed right and left. He
was your employer, therefore what he did for you was
no more than your right. And if the black ever gave
you a present, he would expect an equivalent in
return.

There were exceptions, of course. One day, on
safari, I found a fine sheep before my tent, and on
inquiry I learned that it had been left by a desert
chief who offered by the way of explanation that I
was his best friend. Two days later, a donkey was
delivered by his men. All through that month's
safari I was befriended in this strange way by my
unknown benefactor. It was quite a mystery, particularly since none of the natives of his tribe ever
waited for anything in return, not even a handful of
salt or sugar which they often beg for from caravans
on safari. Osa at last solved the riddle, after some
questioning of Boculy.

"Don't you remember," she said to me one night in
our tent, "that chief you saved from the K.A.R. (the
King's African Rifles)? Well, he's the one."

So it all came back to me. I had been out with
Carl Akeley, the great naturalist, when I came across
a company of K.A.R. who were commandeering
a great number of a chief's cattle. Now they had
a right to do this, for they were on government

business and it was sometimes the only way they could exist. Besides, they paid the chief in dollars. But the native does not always like to be paid in currency. Cattle are coin of the realm to him, and this chief could see no reason in taking his cattle and paying him in cash for which he had no use. And on investigating I found that the guardsmen, who happened to be acting without an officer, were a little too high-handed.

As soon as I discovered this I interceded on behalf of the chief, then sat down and wrote on a piece of red paper that I happened to have in my kit, a lot of high-sounding phrases that threatened with imprisonment any one who ever touched any cattle of this tribe. Of course, it was sheer bluff, for it was anything but official. Still, it took effect, for few of the K.A.R. could read; and the chief for years afterwards showed that piece of red paper to all white men who came through. It was for this service that he now sent so many welcome gifts whenever I went forth in the desert, so perhaps I am partly wrong about their capacity for gratitude. When they do not show it, it is because they are children and take from their white masters without question, as we receive rain or any other blessing from the greatest Master of all.

And certainly they were very kind when we were sick. When Osa had a touch of pneumonia, they stayed up wailing all night thinking that she would die; and in the mornings Phishie, the cook, and his helper would bring the most tempting of dainties and look hurt if she could not eat. Nor could any-one be kinder to his children than a native parent. I have seen a father stop his work to speak kindly to, or play with, his offspring who swarmed about him, while he and his wife repaired their poor grass hut, which was constantly being disturbed by the storms.

I was sitting one night in front of our tent by a waterhole, when I heard noise near the back, and running around, found a hyena walking off with a leather chair I had made. Hastily I pulled off a shoe which I had just unlaced and threw it at him. The hyena dropped the chair and made off with the shoe. I had no sooner ceased cursing at him than three black boys came to me on the run, crying. There was a black boy at our camp subject to epileptic fits and this boy, they told me, had been badly burned. A devil, they said, had visited him and told him to jump in the fire. There was nothing to do but make for camp and here I found the poor boy in a horrible condition. His left leg had been burned to the bone, and he writhed on the dirty straw in the hut moaning horribly.

I did what I could, swabbing out the burns with laboratory cotton, bound him with cloths boiled in hot water and treated with carbolic acid and used unguentine, but the flesh, burned to a crisp, came off in great wads.   Three days and nights, Ndundu, Osa and I worked over him, for all the other natives were afraid of him, as something accursed.   We had to relieve each other, for no man could stand for long that horrible stench of burned and decaying flesh.

The third day, lockjaw set in, and I knew there was no hope.   At midnight he died and next morning I summoned the boys to help with the burial.   With scared looks they edged off from me and ran into the forest.   I did the dreary job alone, putting human pity ahead of impulse.

CHAPTER V

WHEN we were thoroughly established at Lake Paradise we set about our safaris, the native term for expeditions into the field. This was the chief work of our expedition, the purpose of which, as I have said, was to record African wild life in its native haunts in film form.

I picked the various neighborhoods in which I was to work according to the season of the year and the kind of game I was after. Elephants were found right around our camp. We had to go down to the plains to get lions. Waterhole photography was not profitable in wet weather, as water was then too easy for the game to get.

To the untraveled in the wilds of Africa there is little distinction between the species of big game as far as habitat goes. But it must always be remembered that all the varieties of gazelle and antelope, giraffe and warthog, zebra and lions, are to be found in greatest numbers on the plains; while elephants, buffalo, and sometimes rhino are more at home in the

72

A STUDY IN SHADOWS.

I think this picture of two beautiful little Abyssinian bushbuck is one of the most striking I ever made. They were coming up the trail from the lake, within a hundred yards of our home.

IN THE ATTITUDE OF AN ACCOMPLISHED SNEAK.

A striped hyena comes to our kill. After an animal is photographed by flashlight he is blinded for about three minutes. As he runs away, he blunders headlong into trees and bushes in his fright, which grows greater with everything he runs into. Each flash probably terrifies him out of a year's growth.

A HYENA THAT JUMPED BEFORE HE LOOKED.

A sneaky hyena who has got the scent of the meat we have placed in a hole just ahead of him. When the flash went off he jumped into the bush alongside, and had such a hard time getting out that he yelped like a stuck pig.

forests such as those that surrounded our base camp. In the height of the rainy season the latter often journey forth while the waterholes of plain and desert are filled to the brim; but when the worst of the rains are over they troop back again. Boculy, that wise man of the trail, tells me that some rhino never leave the forest, even in the deluge. As for the elephants, they are always glad to get back, once the rains are past, to feed on the wild sweet young ends which they dote on.

As some of our best and most interesting work was done around the waterholes, it might be well for me to describe a day at one.

By June the heat is terrific and dries up all standing water except the larger oases. Our plan is usually to build a blind of thorn bushes. Thorn branches are also put in spots around the water where the camera cannot reach. This keeps the game before us. We go in early and wait for the animals to come. It is tedious work.

I am out at five, eat breakfast, and call the boys to get the cameras. Lunch has been put up by the assistant cook. Osa and I go afoot to the blind, which is some distance away, just as the sun is coming up. It is the most delightful part of the day. During our two or three mile walk we pass hordes of all kinds of game. Hyenas and jackals scurry out of our way. Zebras screech and cough. Lions often roar nearby;

a lion seems to enjoy giving a few defiant roars at daybreak just before he goes to sleep for the day.

We reach the blind in about an hour. The boys have put it together the day before with thornbush, piling up the sides and top to cut out the light. For successful camera work an animal must not be able to detect any movement inside the blind. We go in the blind and set up the camera, arranging the different lenses so that I can get to any of them quickly. The boys push in the thornbush door at the back and hang a blanket over it so no light can filter in. The inside must be dark, with the exception of what comes in from around the lenses in front. Having focussed my lenses on the waterhole I wait until something shows up.

I have a small peep hole arranged from which I can constantly see out. I must keep watching, for the game makes almost no noise as it goes to the water. As my blind is from fifty to seventy yards from the hole, I cannot hear the animals even when they drink.

From nine in the morning until eleven, and from two-thirty to four-thirty is the best time for photographic work, for the light is good. In dry weather the atmosphere seems to catch dust to such an extent that in the late afternoon the light becomes murky. A light rain settles the dust and washes the air. The trouble is that rains are few and far between in the waterhole season. In the rainy season there is so much water that the game does not need to gather at any particular oasis.

Impalla and Grant come and go all day. They walk right to the water without looking around very much. Zebra and oryx come slowly and stop every few feet to look around. Sometimes it takes them two hours to get to water from the time I first see them. This badly wears one's patience.

Giraffe are the most shy of all. They will hang around sometimes for hours without taking a drink. The slightest thing that frightens them sends them off never to return that day. Other game can get many frights but still keep coming back.

The trouble with the giraffe is that he is so painfully awkward. To drink he must spread his four legs stiffly apart and lower his long neck. In that position he is not free to spring away in a gallop. He must scramble for a few vital seconds if there is a lion around. He seems to realize this.

Little game comes along in the morning unless it is a very hot day. On a cloudy day few animals come at any time; but on hot days they come in groups separated by a hundred yards or so. As they amble along they stop now and then and stand dully with their heads down. Apparently the heat makes them sluggish.

Zebra and oryx are always fighting with other members of their own species. These idiots tear around after each other, kicking and snorting and fighting. Of course this stirs up the alkali dust in big clouds. As the fighting animals run through the herds they are snapped at by the others who are much irritated. But hardly has one pair finished their fracas when another pair starts off.

All during the day birds come down to drink. These are fine Kavarando crane, several varieties of storks, heron, hawks, and others. Big vultures come down and stand in the water. They are very picturesque with their fine six-foot spread of wings. For hours they hold their wings out, apparently to cool off their bodies.

When some animal decides to venture to water, all stir. Often I have counted many hundreds of head grouped about. Zebra, especially follow the lead of a courageous one like so many sheep. If he starts to drink then they all try to drink with him. But let one get the slightest start and away go the whole herd in a cloud of dust. Some days the game is so nervous that a fly or a bee will set them all moving. I have never been able to get a big bunch drinking at the same time.

Of course the reason for this nervousness lies in fear of carnivorous animals which are never far away. Lions, leopards and hyenas live on the plains. Their bread and butter consists of zebra and giraffe. None can tell which will be the next victim in the daily slaughter. As a result, when giraffes, zebra or oryx are drinking they prick up their ears at the slight first sound of the camera handle turning. I try to have my machines noiseless, for the slightest click or murmur of gears reaches the ears of these shy animals.

The minute I start turning the handle the animal looks around. But as the sound continues and nothing happens, he goes ahead drinking. When I stop, he gets another start and looks around again. Strange to say, the click of the still camera frightens him more than the whirr of the movie camera.

The larger the herd the less chance there is of getting a picture of common game. The opposite is true of elephants. A single elephant is always on the alert. He knows that the slightest noise may mean danger. But when a herd of elephants come together they are unlikely to stampede. They seem to take it for granted that any noise is made by one of the other elephants. Thus I can always get closer with less danger to a herd of elephants than I can to a single one.

In the long hours at the waterhole one cannot but grow to observe the markings of individual animals.

There was one zebra I used to see time and again. He had a long scar on his back that looked as if it had been caused by a lion.

There was an oryx with only one horn. One Grant had only a single ear. An elephant will sometimes have a broken tusk, or his ear flap will be peculiarly marked. Other beasts you can tell by their offspring, while many have peculiar scars or claw-marks where they have been mauled by leopards or lions and yet through fleetness of foot and good luck have escaped.

Now comes a long line of fifteen warthogs in single file. They all trot along at about the same speed, their tails in the air; they have a comical self-satisfied look about them. They stir up a lot of dust with their little feet. I hope they will come close to me; but, as luck has it, when they reach within ten feet of the water they swerve off and trot away without changing speed or seeming to be frightened. "Water-hole luck" Osa calls it.

I can always tell when ostriches are coming up even before I see them. Our animals pay no attention to different species of other four-legged game. They rub shoulders and all seem to be friends. But the minute an ostrich comes along, the ranks part. I have never seen an ostrich kick at another animal. Yet he seems to be feared. Also he is fearless. When he starts for water and there is other game in the path he never swerves or goes around it. He marches along with a slow dignified gait and the game makes way for him.

One of my troubles is from animals coming up behind the blind. They get my scent and frighten away the game in front. It wouldn't be so bad if they went completely away. The trouble is they just back off a hundred yards or so and keep the other game in a nervous state for hours.

At 1 P.M. I have lunch. For an hour or so I doze The heat is usually pretty awful. Like the animals outside it depresses me. They don't feel like drinking and I don't feel like photographing. With the sun directly overhead, the light is not right anyway.

About 2:30 the animals start again for water. Around 4 o'clock they drink more and frighten less than at any time of the day. I suppose it is because many have put their thirst off all day and have decided to take a chance even if there is danger. Unfortunately, by this time the sun is getting low and shining at such an angle that it makes a yellow light that is bad for pictures.

I leave the blind about 6 P.M. and get back to camp near 7. Meanwhile my boys have started from camp at 5:30. Suku sends them off when our big alarm clock rings. They stop on a hill top near the blind and wait for me to blow my whistle to show that I am ready to leave.

I cannot leave anything in the blind on account of baboons. They are so curious and inquisitive that they run off with anything they can carry. Hyenas and jackals will take anything made of leather during the night.

As time went on we gave names to those waterholes which we visited most. We usually named them in Swahili so that the boys could identify them when we gave directions.

The one we called Wistonia was not far from our base camp. It was perhaps, the most beautiful of all. Great rocks, fifty feet high, surrounded it, showing beautiful hues varying from rose-reds to deep volcanic blue-black; facing the opening was a valley half a mile in length, richly embroidered, after the rains, with emerald green and rainbow-like flowers. The valley itself was cut by a ravine, or donga, with green swamp rushes and vegetation in the bottom and ferns and tropical vines growing up its sides.

The waterhole, bulwarked by three cliffs, was about seventy-five feet wide and fed out into a swift-racing stream that skipped down the donga in a succession of little silver rapids until it disappeared from sight around a bend in the ravine.

When we discovered this we followed one of the streams as it sped down a green-sided channel; and everywhere we went, we found other swift racing little streams coursing down ledges until they also fell in a succession of rapids and white waterfalls. Where all these little rivers came from we could not tell; but they were delightful, sometimes pausing in their

TOPI ON THE PLAINS OF NORTHWEST TANGANYIKA.

The topi is almost good looking—he has a kindly eye, a beautiful velvet brown skin, and horns that would be graceful if they were not so thick. But his big kongoni-like head spoils his looks entirely. Note the zebra in the background.

A Brazen Member of the Beggars' Guild.

A maribou stork in the top of a thorn tree.   These storks were not easily frightened and would patiently sit in the trees about
the camp, waiting for the feed the cook threw away.   This is a typical scene in the game country in Tanganyika.

precipitous flight to broaden out into pools where water lilies floated, butterflies seemed to hang suspended, and innumerable little orange gold finches sang. Finally they increased in number until they formed a real little river, only to plunge again over rose-red and violet rocks into still larger water falls.

I shall never forget the moonlit night we spent there at the Wistonia hole; just Osa and I, in our blind. About ten o'clock two full-grown rhinos came down and drank for fifteen minutes without stopping. These animals certainly have large tanks in their insides, for they drink without once pausing and the noise they make during the operation is like that of a Chinaman eating soup. This pair got through drinking, turned and went away as if they had important business elsewhere.

Not ten minutes later a big rhino came down all alone for a drink. He consumed gallons and gallons of water and then, like the earlier ones, briskly departed. About midnight I was asleep, when Osa gently awakened me. I heard a scraping of feet and stones falling on the trail. A moment later buffalo came into view. They poured down by the score, crowding about, sniffing the air and advancing to the water so closely packed that they pushed one another into it. Altogether there were over two hundred drinking there at one time and the noisy quenching of their thirst must have been audible for a mile in the still night.

I went back to sleep again; but Osa can never sleep while in a blind. She is always too excited and curious about what is going to happen next. She wakened me again about 4 A.M. when a herd of elephants came to water from behind us and caught our scent before they had their drink. They snorted and trumpeted for half an hour in expressing their annoyance. But in the end they went away without touching the water.

Another night we spent together at a waterhole we had named "Old Lady." That time we had a good scare from a leopard that became too curious, but finally got rid of the fellow without using our guns.

Near the edge of the forest and the foot of the slope that gave way to the great desert below our lake, was another waterhole that was particularly fascinating. It was really more than one waterhole, rather a chain of pools, fed by leakage from the big lake, which probably has many outlet passages running underground.

One day in a great mimosa tree by the largest pool, the head of the chain, we built a blind, and here we spent the whole of four nights to see what we could see. The first night, the rain came down in buckets; our tarpaulin covering on the roof slipped and since even in blinds we usually change to pajamas, we were drenched to the skin and huddled miserably in wet blankets and sheets. All around us we could hear crackling of branches disjointed by the wind. There were other reports more terrifying at first, for the soil here is volcanic. As a result the roots of the trees are near the surface; and in the heavy rains, when the soil is washed away, the trees fall right and left as if under the axes of hordes of invisible foresters.

We were repaid, however, for all our misery when the following days turned out fair and we had abundant opportunities to take pictures of and study the animals. The bushbuck came down often, hurriedly as do all the gazelle and antelope, fearing, no doubt, attack at any moment from lions and leopards. Centuries have taught them discretion and they do not linger long, but simply drink and hurry away. Little jackals came on a dog-like trot, sniffing the air. Ugly hyenas slouched in with wicked grins and that ugly gait of theirs caused by their long forelegs and short hindlegs. Sometimes at night several would stand and snarl at the moon; and, if you listened attentively, the yelps seemed to take on an individuality, ranging from gruff growls to whimpers, varied with the most impudent and bloodcurdling of staccato laughter.

Week in, week out, I was very busy with my flashlight work near the waterholes around the base camp or in its vicinity. Cameras were carefully concealed in brush near the trails and wires strung across the paths. By a device consisting of small disks on springs, the contact of an animal's foot with the wires would set off my flash.

At first we had little success. We got things like little gennet cats which are cunning enough ordinarily, but seemed to be moved to investigate our mechanism. However, these were not the fellows we came after.

The night of my first successful flashlight I was in bed when we heard the report and the boys came running in filled with excitement. Two rhinos had set off the flash with results that turned out later to be splendid. Of course the discharge scared away all game in the vicinity for some time. But five hours later the flash went off again, released by some bird or other small animal. To make matters worse the glare and thud of the explosion stampeded a herd of elephants that had wandered in.

At some of the waterholes where we had placed our flashes we found that birds had flown into the wire at such a terrific speed that everything was broken and we had no pictures; again elephants' feet had twisted the wires and snapped them; and such pictures as we took of waterfowl were vague and blurred because the birds, after striking the wire, vibrated like gyroscopes. Finally, even the gennet cats grew wise; for instead of snapping at the meat which was hung from a cross wire suspended between two poles and which served as bait to lead our quarry to the disk spring which would start the flash, they climbed up the poles and across the wire and there devoured the meat. Once or twice we caught them at it; and it was funny to see them like tightrope walkers, cautiously making their way across the rope, every once in a while pausing and making their little noses go like rabbits, sniffing the air as if for danger.

Sometimes for my flashlight work on the beasts of prey I had to use bait to supplement the waterhole lure. I remember one night waiting with Osa in a blind near one of the marsh-like holes where we had placed a dead zebra. Before sunset forty of my boys had dragged the carcass about for a couple of hours in order to leave a scent for the lions to follow.

Then we took into our boma the electric wire leading to the charge of magnesium powder we had placed behind our camera near the bait. With us we had only our guns and an electric torch.

Until ten o'clock nothing showed up except hundreds of zebra and all the common game that we had kept away while working about during the day. Five giraffes stood under a tree nearby and nibbled at the tender young buds among the thorns.

At ten o'clock, I was asleep. As the bright moonlight was reflected by the sandy alkali soil it seemed almost like day. Suddenly I was awakened by a gentle push in my ribs and Osa warned me in a whisper not to make any noise. I slowly raised up and looked out through our peep hole. There was a full-grown maneless lion standing near the zebra kill. He was a beauty, his head moving in every direction very slowly as if to see that everything was all right before starting to eat.

It was a fine sight. But the lion was not in the exact position I wanted him. Also his head was too far down. When he moved a little nearer I whistled gently. At this he looked around but not far enough. Then I turned my pocket flashlight on him. Now he looked directly at me, but not in alarm. At this instant I pressed the button of my flash. It went off with a loud boom. The lion was temporarily blinded and sprang wildly into the thorn fence we had laid to guide him before the camera. The photograph turned out beautifully.

All waterhole work, night or day, was not as simple as that just described. For instance, some of the nicest pools were made dangerous by arrows of the native tribe of Ndoros. These shafts were set up in such a way that the animals coming to drink would let go a string that would cause a hidden bow to shoot the arrow direct at the drinking animal. A dangerous trap for man or beast, especially if the arrows were poisoned.

Not always would the game behave just as we wanted it to. In one pool we were after hippos and had failed to get good film. Unexpectedly we came on a huge crocodile fast asleep with long jaws gaping wide open. I set up the Akeley camera and told Osa to go to a point above me and when I gave the word to shoot near his head, but not to hit him. When everything was ready, I signalled to her and started to turn the crank of my machine. Osa did as she was told and shot within a few inches of the reptile. He didn't even move! Then slowly he closed his jaws. I told Osa to shoot again; she did; but the crocodile slept on. Finally we gave up our plan as a bad job and started down to chase the lazy fellow into the water with rocks. But just then a monster hippopotamus which had been asleep under a rocky ledge, splashed noisily away in shallow water. We rushed back to our camera, but it was too late.

CHAPTER VI

WILDERNESS FOLK

ONE of the ways I used to while away the tedium
of my long hours at the waterholes was to make
notes on the creatures which came down to drink.
The more wild animals I come in contact with, the
more human they seem to me. The camel is a
peevish old woman; the elephant a scholarly gentleman; the giraffe a born aristocrat; the lion a sportsman; zebras are just plain rowdies; the ostrich is
a bully; the leopard an assassin, and so on. I remember one camel which used to be the leader in
our column on safari. I suppose the old fellow I have
in mind was past his prime. But for a camel he was
in good health and well treated. He had food and
water when he needed them, and he had no sores or
disease.

Yet he used to start the day with a long
lamentation. He would chew his cud between
wheezy cries; then suddenly stop and make a sharp
noise between a whinny and a sneeze.

When his native keeper came along to load him up
he invariably snapped at the man. When the load

ELEPHANTS ASLEEP AT NOON.

Taken outside the Lake Paradise forests. It was amusing to watch them trying to crowd under trees that were often too small to give shade to a single elephant—yet we have seen thirty of these great beasts under one little tree.

MORE ELEPHANTS IN THE SAME REGION.

Note the tusks which have been broken by being used as levers in breaking down trees. Elephants like to eat the tender young buds and shoots at the top of the trees, which they pull down with their trunks, getting a good leverage on the tree with their tusks. We have seen this happen many times. Some hunters say elephants break their tusks by fighting, but we are confident this is not true.

was put on the saddle he groaned as if in great pain. And when he got the order to rise, emphasized by a stiff toe prod, he would snort and cry out as if he were being beaten unmercifully.

In the meantime the other camels were going through their own expressions of misery. Probably they took their cue from the leader. The exchanges, no doubt, ran something like this:

"Oh, what a terrible life!"

"Yes, and such heavy loads they put on us."

"My back, oh, my back; how my hump aches!"

"Well, it hasn't anything on my hind legs."

"I suppose we're going miles and miles today."

"Yes, and it's terribly hot!"

"Oh, oh, oh!"

"Oh, oh, oh!"

After a performance of this sort it's a pleasure to have dealings with lions. I shall tell more fully later how Carl Akeley helped us find a little valley where the lions had never been disturbed. Then for the first time I got a clear picture of lion personality. Eleven unconcerned lions were right out in plain sight, loafing around in the grass and panting with the heat. Some were asleep; one old male rolled over with his four paws in the air while we were there.

Slowly we approached, taking pictures as we went. It seemed impossible that the animals would continue to lie right out there in the open and neither charge nor retreat. But that is exactly what they did.

Finally we were only a few feet from a gorgeous old warrior. He raised his head and glanced disdainfully at us. He seemed to say: "They're queer-looking creatures, but it's too hot to investigate them; anyway, I'm not hungry."

About this time a plump female emerged from the forest some distance away and came over to where her friends were dozing. One by one she awakened them with sly digs of her forepaw. They were annoyed at her idea of fun, but did not fight back.

One lion rose and walked off. He strode with slow dignity as if he had some deliberate business in mind. He did not even glance our way, though I am sure he kept us in sight out of the corner of his eye.

In action the lion is 100 per cent in earnest. When he is hungry he goes straight to a herd of zebra or giraffe and singles out his animal without delay; often he stampedes the herd, and one is left behind. He kills it swiftly and surely. At once he eats his fill. He sleeps but twenty or thirty feet away from the carcass. When he awakes and can eat some more, he again sets to work. Meanwhile the carrion of the jungle keep their distance.

In combat the lion is knightly in his courage and fierce tenacity. I have seen him face terrible odds against a score of natives armed with long spears and shields. The first burning sting of steel in his flesh shows him what he is up against. He has all the wide plain in which to flee. Yet he continues the attack, roaring his defiance, until he falls, still facing his enemy, his body pierced with a dozen fatal thrusts.

I think the hyena offers the greatest contrast to the lion. This slinking animal is cowardly, cruel, selfish, unsocial and in a dozen other ways contemptible. I have seen a hyena run through a flock of defenseless goats at night, hamstringing one after another as he went for no reason on earth other than the vicious joy of torturing them. Sometimes at a waterhole he will break animals' backbones or otherwise mutilate them and leave them to die.

A hyena will lie in the bushes and spring out for the young goats as they pass down the trail. He will do this even when he is not hungry. He is a born murderer. A hyena is a coward and a sneak. I remember meeting one unexpectedly near our camp. His head was bleeding. Rarely have I seen such an expression of ignominy on any creature. He had been stealing out of one of our food boxes, and got it caught about his head.

One day we had just started to walk away from camp when two hyenas came along. They didn't see us at all. They were laughing away, like a pair of fools, just as if they were two traveling men and one had told a good joke. It was the first time I had ever actually seen a hyena laugh. It was so funny that our boys shook with repressed mirth. Osa and I nearly split our sides. As the natives have a somewhat anæmic sense of humor, the contagious nature of the hyena's cackle may be judged from this early morning incident.

The ostrich is a strutter. His stiff-legged walk adds to the air of false dignity about him. The big black male is a great dude. The female is a fitting mate. She is continually preening herself. She rises slightly on her toes and flaps her wings, for all the world like a prim old lady rising and settling herself in a chair.

Few members of the bird or animal kingdom are wider awake to the proximity of trouble or danger, or more quickly hie themselves to safe ground when they decide it is time to move, than ostriches. I think the tradition that the ostrich buries its head in the sand on the approach of an enemy rose from the fact that it often gets water by poking its long beak down into the ground and sucking.

I believe I have told how ordinary quadrupeds seem to be afraid of the ostrich. I have never seen him strike out with his heavy foot, but many a time I have watched herds of zebra and giraffe and others break ranks voluntarily to let the long-legged bird through.

The funniest sight in the world is to see an ostrich come down off his "high horse." I remember once when we were slowly working our heavy trucks up from Nairobi toward Lake Paradise over trails soggy with the long rains. Through the light growth on one side we could see a group of ostriches peering at the strange visitors to their domain. Presently their curiosity got the better of them. They began to run ahead and cross the trail in order to get an unobstructed view of our cars. The trail was deep with mud and puddles. As each of the big birds reached it he centered his gaze on us. The first one got over all right. The second was squarely in the center of the trail when his feet slipped and—splasho —he fell into the middle of a mudhole! One after another the idiotic birds rushed out and sprawled in the muck with a great fluttering of wings and scrambling of feet. At this sight of ruined ostrich pride Osa and I roared with laughter.

The African wart hog is just plain pig; he looks like a pig, tastes like a pig and usually acts the way I think a pig would act if he were continually hunted by lions, leopards, wild dogs and natives. He has long tusks with which he does great battle with his own kind. But they are of small help when he is set upon by one of the big cats or a pack of wild dogs.

In consequence of his unhappy lot the wart hog has developed a distinct inferiority complex. He looks enormously startled when you meet him. He sticks his little tail stiffly up in the air and gives vent to snorts and squeals of fright. He darts through the underbrush and makes headlong speed for the nearest ant-bear hole.

The hole of the ant bear is the wart hog's only safe refuge. These holes are only a foot or so in diameter and many feet deep. Once down them, the wart hog is safe from all but man, and he won't come out even if you dig down to him. But how he settles his score with his sharp-clawed host is something I have never found out. There may be some division of spoils about which I shall forever remain in ignorance. I think the truth is that the ant bear is never there, since he digs hundreds of holes looking for food and probably doesn't go back to them.

I like elephants. They are the fine, upstanding middle-class citizenry of the jungle. They attend to their own business. They fight little among themselves, make good, intelligent parents and have a real instinct of tribal loyalty.

Once when I found it necessary to shoot to save my life from a charging elephant the big animal was mortally wounded, I wanted to fell him to save him from suffering. But while I was getting ready to fire again, two of his companions came on either side of the wounded warrior as if to support him as he tottered pitifully into the forest.

I have seen a mother elephant lambaste her toto with her trunk, push it gently into column when it was falling with weariness, and squirt mud over it from her trunk when it was crying from the oppressive heat of the plains.

There is often something comical about an elephant because of its size and its indifference to what goes on about it when not alarmed. I remember one big fellow that had been feeding through the branches of a small grove of saplings. Suddenly he became so drowsy that he ambled to the nearest tree and leaned against it for a nap. He slept until suddenly my wind reached him and he roused himself enough to waddle away into the brush.

When fully roused the elephant is thoroughly vindictive. He apparently has no desire to kill save when in a state of intense indignation at being intruded upon when he has been bothering no one in the world.

Few animals respond to leadership as does the elephant.

One day I was sitting in a blind with Osa waiting to get a picture. Soon we saw a group of shadowy forms come through the trees across the little open space that separated them from the waterhole.

As one elephant is always ahead on such occasions, you can't get a photograph of the herd; it stands back.

On this occasion, as usual, the leader walked cautiously down toward the water while his twenty or so companions, some yards to the rear, awaited his verdict: one of the finest samples of animal prudence I have ever seen.

After a few moments he went back to his comrades and stood by them for a little while. Then he returned to the vicinity of the blind. He repeated this action half a dozen times. All the while the others stood perfectly quiet, as if they reposed full confidence in the old fellow. None showed the slightest impatience to get the drink that all must have yearned for after the scorching day just ended.

Once another elephant came down while the first one waited with the line. But his verdict seemed also to be that trouble was near. Finally the leader went back to his people for a last time. This time all faded away into the jungle.

The rhinoceros is a big, fat, stupid old idiot. He is always fighting, always in a bad humor, always grunting, always looking for trouble. I think he has the least desirable personality of any of the big beasts.

I don't believe that the average rhino has a friend in the world, not even among his own kind. Rhinos don't go about in herds or mingle with other animals. When I meet them they seem to be always either fighting among themselves or making ready to fight us. On numerous occasions I have been treed by an angry rhino.

RESTING IN THE FIELD.

"Us" taking time out between pictures while a band of Meru blacks looks on.

AT HOME ON SAFARI.

This double tent with the outside fly is the usual tent for African camp life. The space between the fly and the tent allows a cool passage of air, and makes the tent more comfortable in the rains. From the fly runs a veranda fly that makes a comfortable shade for lounging about. We took the latter off so that the inside of the tent could be photographed.

Once when Osa went to investigate a rhino I told her to ride off down another trail on my mule. The first thing she knew she came plump on the big beast! Her mule was terrified; so was the rhino. Both of them started to run together. Fortunately they came to a place where the trail branched and the two crazy creatures diverged.

A female rhino must make a poor mother-in-law. She keeps her grumbling young one with her until it is as big as she.

I think all rhinos must wake up in the morning in a bad humor. As a sample of their petulance I recall one night when we were camping in tents on the side of a hill. Saunderson was below Osa and me at the edge of our line. Right in the middle of the night an old rhino came along and stuck her head through Saunderson's tent flap.

There was only one thing for the startled man to do. He kicked the intruding lady in the face and scrambled out through the back of the tent. Whereupon the "lady" charged. She took tent and pole off with her at a gallop down the trail into the forest.

The hippopotamus belongs to the same class of large animals as do the elephant and rhino. But if the elephant is a scholarly gentleman and the rhino a thundering old grouch, the hippo can be personified only as the sort of fat fellow who sits on the back porch without his collar of hot afternoons while his wife takes in washing for a living.

There is nothing more soothing to the nerves than to see a balloon-like hippo half submerged in a nice muddy river chewing its cud as if nothing in the wide world mattered. Indeed, nothing does matter to these placid beasts so long as there is water and fodder enough to go around.

A hippopotamus is very comical when frightened. Like an obese ignoramus not used to being disturbed, he loses his head in emergency and is quite incapable of doing anything about the danger which threatens him.

I remember coming upon a pair in a big river pool one hot afternoon. Immediately they submerged like a pair of fat submarines. I think they must have doubled their feet up under them for the water was very shallow. But they could not stay under the water for any length of time, since all hippos must come up to breathe.

Sure enough, in a few minutes two wide snouts came panting and snorting to the scummy surface. When the beady eyes discovered that I was still there a great commotion ensued. More diving and snorting and frantic fat efforts.

The encounter ended tamely enough when both beasts got out of breath and decided that it was no use to scramble any longer. They simply settled down in the middle of the pool with snouts and eyes just above the surface and waited calmly for the end —whatever that might be—only hoping against hope that they'd be left in peace.

The smaller four-legged animals are in some ways less distinctive in their human traits than the big ones. Yet they present many exaggerated human characteristics.

The African wild buffalo, for instance, is exactly like a man who is always being stampeded by the latest rumor. He is continually and unnecessarily on the alert; not sensibly, like the cat family, but in a silly, apprehensive way that must take much of the joy out of his life. He will graze for a few moments in a natural manner; then up goes his head as he feels the wind. There may be no enemy within many miles, and his herd may not have been molested by man or by beasts of prey for months. It makes no difference; he is always nervous and ready to enjoy a panic at the slightest provocation. I have seen buffalo at the waterhole in this mood when all the other animals were as quiet and peaceful as a Sunday-school picnic.

One interesting thing about the buffalo is the determined way in which he protects his own clan when an enemy appears. At the first warning he joins his brothers in a curved line, heads to the front. Calves and cows take position behind. In this formation, with horns lowered and forelegs pawing the ground, the animals present a truly formidable defense.

Perhaps it is this same nervousness that makes the buffaloes such aggressive animals. I know of several people they have killed; they make an awful mess of the body when they murder. Of course the buffaloes are prey for the carnivores, but their wiry build and combative disposition make them a tough meal to secure. My warning to strangers is always that the buffalo is one of the most dangerous customers on the trail. He is a cutthroat from the word go.

The wildebeest is one wild animal that has little or no personality. He is strictly "cow." He chews his cud and lies down when in a placid mood. At other times he is like a colt in a paddock, running about and kicking his heels in the air. Like the buffalo, he is very much on the alert. And, like many a human being, he dashes away from the slightest alarm, only to draw up after a wild gallop and wonder what it's all about.

The zebra is an animal with an interesting personality. He is silly and stupid. He often seems to stampede for the very deviltry of it and is a great hand to stampede other game. He is a first-class rowdy, always snapping and quarreling among his own kind, which roam in big herds. As two fighters dash through the herd, others turn and snap angrily at them, often kicking out with a vengeance and no little accuracy.

One scrawny little fellow used to come down near our blind day after day. As he was too young to be alone, I concluded that his mother must have been killed by a lion or leopard. Zebras, you know, are the lion's favorite food. This particular youngster was frail and terrified. Once for three days straight he came near the waterhole, but was too frightened to drink. I suppose he may have seen his mother killed. Finally he could stand it no longer. Trembling in every limb, he walked right into the water and drank until it seemed he would burst.

Like the zebra, the giraffe is also an appetizing dish for the lion. This is distressing when one sees how kind and gentle this creature is. I look on the giraffe as the true aristocrat of the jungle. His manners are always impeccable; his bearing is dignified, and his bearing towards other beasts is full of the utmost good-natured tolerance.

The great trouble in the giraffe's life is his grotesque figure. His legs are long and stiff, and his neck is limber. He has no way to make a single sound of warning or complaint and nature has endowed him with no practicable means of defense. I have heard it said that a giraffe can put up quite a fight with his forelegs, but I seriously doubt it. He just isn't built for fighting.

Time and again my heart has been wrung by the sight of a giraffe that has become prey to one of the big flesh-eating animals. Once I came upon one with the flesh ripped from its haunches, dying. There was no sign of a fight. Apparently the lion had left but a few moments before, as the animal's big brown eyes were not yet glazed by death.

Another time I came upon a mother giraffe and her baby which must have been born only the night before. I was able to get right up to the pair because the baby was not afraid and refused to follow its mother. She must have been expecting us to attack her any moment but she stuck it out and didn't leave until her infant would go with her.

The leopard is a killer. He is the gunman of the jungle. Also he is full of mystery: he makes little or no noise in his activities, and he charges unexpectedly —a sinister shadow from nowhere, bringing death with his final leap.

The leopard is not so dignified as the lion, nor is he quite so sneaky as the hyena. He is a solitary worker, without companions and without the trust of any other animal in the jungle.

He does not have the courage always to eat in the open as the lion does. He kills and carries his prey away. He will carry up a tree an antelope weighing half again as much as himself, lugging the carcass over his shoulder as a highwayman might carry a bag of loot.

One instance will show the deadly nature of this fellow. I was some distance from camp with our truck one day. Rattray of the British settlement was with us. Osa shot a zebra, but unfortunately only wounded it.

"Let me get it for you," suggested Rattray, who hopped out while he was speaking. He took his gun and started off in the direction of the wounded animal.

The zebra had fallen near some brush. Rattray said afterward that the first thing he saw was a grey shadow crouched behind the neck of the animal. The next thing he knew this shadow was sweeping toward him over the ground almost with the speed of a bird. It was absolutely noiseless as it came. He knew at once it was a full-grown leopard charging him. He fired and missed. The next cartridge of his double-barreled piece failed to go off. In another instant the leopard was upon him with its fangs at his throat.

When we rescued the poor chap his clothes and flesh were ripped horribly from head to foot. It was two years before he finally recovered from this assault.

On the trail of lions and leopards we always find jackal and hyena. The natives say that the former are special friends of lions and help them to find their prey. I do know that I have seen a jackal quietly wait a few feet away for a lion to have his fill of a carcass and then come up for a meal without objection from the larger animal. This, the natives say, is the way the lion pays the jackal for his help.

But the wretched hyena does not stand in so well. I have seen one slink up when he thought the lion had gone away. Scarcely had he begun to feed when the big cat was after him. Once under such circumstances I saw a lion overtake a hyena and administer a blow that must have maimed the scalawag for life.

Around our Lake Paradise home we have thousands of baboons. Not all are in one herd, but in smaller groups or clans. In a way they are the most entertaining of all the animals we know, because they are grotesquely like human beings.

They are forever screeching and rowing and fighting among themselves when they turn in at night. Apparently there is a new series of combats every evening to see who will get the best crotches and branches for sleeping on.

In one of our nearest groups there is a big male whom I have come to know because he seems so to resent the presence of Osa and me in the neighborhood. He chatters and shakes his long arms when he sees us, and retreats, hurling maledictions on our heads.

The baby baboons are very cute, but lead a terrible life, being mauled all over the place by their elders.

Wherever they go or whatever they do they are cuffed and abused not only by parents but also by distant friends and relatives.

There are many other animals we know and like and live with or near from day to day. And all have distinct personalities. Not all, however, do we know well enough to see in them those fascinating traits that make life in Africa so full of charm. For instance there is the happy gentle gazelle, with its tail that is always wagging. We had a pet one for a while until he drifted away into the jungle and never came back. There are the birds and the rare animals, such as the okapi; there are the strange reptiles, not by any means so repulsive as is often thought.

After all, man, about whom our thoughts so closely revolve, is in God's eyes just another animal.

CHAPTER VII

OUR BACKYARD CIRCUS

ONE day at Paradise my Meru carpenter came running to the door of my laboratory very much excited and shouting in Swahili: "Elephants! Elephants!"

This wasn't exactly news, for the woods about us were full of the big animals. But I grabbed my big Akeley camera and tripod and followed the man to the back of the shack, hoping as usual to get something out of the ordinary. There in the open scrub about two hundred yards away were fifteen elephants, several bulls, four or five cows, three half-grown animals and two babies. They were all just feeding along as comfortably as could be.

Of course, I started to grind out film. When I had turned down about two hundred feet what was my surprise to see Osa duck up between me and the elephants and shout: "What are you doing? Have you gone crazy?" There she was, weeding her strawberries in the garden not a hundred yards from the herd of wild elephants and blissfully ignorant of its presence. Our calling back and forth, and the movements of the boys about the camp finally caused the

OVERLOOKING THE KAISOOT DESERT.

The mounds are extinct volcanoes. Lake Paradise overlooks a vast tract of country whose lonely grandeur
I have seldom seen equalled anywhere in the world.

A Scene Near Lake Paradise.

We had pitched camp here, near the Abyssinian border of British East Africa. This whole countryside is unique for its desolate and beautiful scenery.

beasts to move on down toward the lake; but not before I had another good view filmed of elephant life.

Years ago in Kansas as a small boy, long before I ever dreamed I'd go to Africa to live, I watched the big greyish black beasts waddle by on circus day with their curious shuffling walk. They looked so slow and stupid, so indifferent to what went on about them, so grotesquely out of place amid the trumpery of civilization, that even as a small boy I wondered vaguely what they might be like in their own native haunts.

As I grew older I picked up the traditional beliefs about the elephant. I learned to think of him as a mixture of viciousness and sagacity when he was aroused, and as a profoundly dumb brute when left to his own devices. I knew he was trained at hauling teak in India and at doing meaningless tricks in America.

I heard many tales of the elephant's power of memory and desire for revenge. "Don't feed the elephant" was a sign we all knew was based on the fact the beast might become violent if given red pepper instead of peanuts. An elephant killed a man in Brooklyn who burned his tusk with his lighted cigar. "Alice," one of the New York Zoo collection vented her anger by rushing into the Reptile House and throwing to the concrete floor glass show cases filled with poisonous snakes. And so on.

To the lay eye, the African elephant seems the same animal as the Indian elephant, which is the species always seen in circuses. The reason for this choice is that the Hindu for centuries has domesticated elephants for purposes of labor and transportation. An African native shrinks from such intimacy with the huge quadrupeds. Hence the African elephant has long had cause to fear man, if only through constant threat of the ivory hunters.

We don't shoot elephants or anything else at Lake Paradise. Our chief work consists solely of filming wild game in its natural habitat. As a result there has grown up among the elephant herds in our vicinity none of the terror and vindictiveness so often reported from India where herds attack native villages *en masse* and do terrible damage.

Two incidents, while somewhat extreme, illustrate what I mean. About twenty years ago a train on the railway in Burma was attacked by an elephant. The engineer whistled as he took a grade. A big bull elephant feeding nearby interpreted the blast as a challenge. He loudly trumpeted his acceptance of the invitation to do battle. He lowered his head and made for the oncoming train. Once on the tracks he met it almost exactly head-on. The engineer had no time to stop. Probably he was so dumbfounded by the sight of the huge beast galloping towards him that he was powerless to act. Engine and elephant collided with a terrific crash. The latter's massive head was caved in and he was instantly killed. But the momentum of his enormous carcass weighing several tons did its work. The engine was derailed and its front end crushed to a shapeless mass.

Contrast the atmosphere around Lake Paradise where Osa rushed in one morning from her garden with flushed face and flashing eyes exclaiming:

"Oh, I think it's mean of them!"

"Who?" I snapped, wondering angrily if the natives had been misbehaving.

"Those elephants. They've been at my vegetable garden again!"

Wild elephants, too; wild and free as the mammoth and mastodon were in their day, and nearly as big.

As I said before, I think our guide Boculy knows more about elephants than any man living. He could study a single elephant track and usually in a few minutes tell me just how many there were in the herd, where they had gone, what they were doing and what we should do to find and photograph them.

He was an absolutely tireless fellow. Indeed he never could understand any of the rest of us getting tired. Time and again he walked us for three or four hours up and down hills and across rough sun-scorched stones, until we would call a halt in sheer exhaustion.

He was never at a loss for a reply if I tried to hurry

him. When we halted in case we had not already found game, I would usually say, "Now let's go where the game has gone, Boculy."

To which he would invariably reply: "But Master, they are not there."

He had a lot of queer maxims. If he failed for a considerable time to find elephants he would say one of three things was the cause:

"Shauri ako" . . . Business caused by you (the white man).

"Shauri Muunga" . . . Business caused by God.

"Shauri mvua." . . . Business caused by rain.

When he made up his mind that we were not find-ing game for one of these reasons he usually insisted on giving up the hunt for the day and would not look any further.

Early in our stay I explained to Boculy how I planned to do a lot of photographic work of animals from the protection of blinds. This, I told him, would give me a chance to observe them in an undisturbed state. But he only grinned and said something about my not knowing what I was saying. Sure enough he proved to be correct. For the finest films of elephants which I took were made right out in the open.

I had many a lesson in trailing elephants from Boculy without his knowing it. One day he walked along looking at some tracks which were at least

NDOROBO HUNTERS.

These hunters came to tell us of game outside the forests. We were many months in getting their confidence so that we could talk to them, but after they became used to us they would often bring us news of game migrations in return for salt and sugar. These Ndorobo are not of any one tribe. In fact, every tribe has its Ndorobo people who break away from the tribal laws and wander over Africa, living by the bow and arrow and spear.

A LUMBWA WARRIOR.

These Lumbwa are a cast-off from the Nandi tribe. They are not afraid of anything on earth and would rather fight than eat. I have found that they have more character than any African tribe I have ever met.

twenty-four hours old. He was talking to himself
most of the time. Now and then he would stop and
look at the track and point in the direction he evidently thought the animal might have gone. He
would then pick a twig or leaf up and name the hour
it had been chewed on. Presently he was tracking
over short grass where there wasn't a single sign
visible to my untrained eye, not a smear of mud or
dirt left by the animal's foot. Finally he would
take scent like a bloodhound, go off like an arrow and
in a few minutes turn around with a grin, pointing to
the elephant he had been following. It was uncanny.

Sometimes he had arguments with himself when he
didn't come on the elephants as soon as he thought he
ought to. He'd stop and look at the ground and say,
"yes, yes." Then shake his head and slowly say,
"No, no." At last he would suddenly exclaim,
"*Yes!*" with conviction and we would be off to find
another herd of elephants before an hour passed.

When the time came for us seriously to take the
trail we didn't have to go far for a great deal of our
best film. I simply talked things over with Boculy,
decided on how and where we should operate and
organized my safari, or field expedition, to suit.

There was one particular herd I had been wanting
to get at for months. It wasn't large; but there were
some young ones in it which I wanted to photograph. We finally set off after it fully equipped

with plenty of porters for our gear and with food for about two weeks' travel.

We camped near the edge of the jungle after a march of nearly twenty miles. About five the next morning Boculy woke us. He whispered something about elephants in my ear. I hurried out of the tent and saw ten elephants walking quietly along about four hundred yards away. Two were so young that they looked like Christmas toys. They were toddling, bumping up against their mothers and stopping and turning around just like children on a street. Each mother would turn around every now and then and slap her offspring with her trunk. This would make the little fellow squeal and he would trot along obediently again.

Two more were about six months old. They were very solemn, even more so than the grown-up ones. But every now and then they would get bored with the march they were on and start to wander off. A severe grunt from one of the older ones would bring them back into line.

We hustled around and got our cameras ready. It was still too dark to photograph but I thought we could follow without the animals seeing us, especially as the wind was from them to us.

Just before the sun came up the whole line walked along the top of a small hill. They came to a halt. Silhouetted against the sky they made a wonderful picture, a picture of which I have often dreamed. I had seen films of camels silhouetted against the sky. At last I could make one of elephants. I lost no time in doing so.

We left camp after breakfast. About an hour later we were stopped suddenly by Boculy, who stepped softly back with his hand raised for silence. Ahead of us were seven elephants, just beside the trail. I ran back a few steps and motioned for the camera boys to hurry. We set up the cameras as quickly as we could, but the elephants walked into the brush, feeding as they went.

I had just about decided that they were going to have a sleep under cover when I heard a noise on the other side of the trail. More elephants had come up. I crept ahead and saw three. They, too, were settling down for a sleep in the dark forest where it would be impossible to make pictures. Boculy was annoyed with me. He could never understand that I needed plenty of light for pictures. He thought my magic box ought to be able to see in the dark as well as in the light, certainly if it were magic enough to reproduce moving creatures months later.

We didn't dare disturb the elephants. Had they stampeded us we never could have escaped them. There were no trees to climb and their anger at being waked up would have been uncontrollable. I had the cameras gathered up and hurried my party along the trail, hoping that we should meet some elephants which were not yet bound for bed. The heat probably was making them all sleepy. Hardly had we started when we ran into three more right ahead of us.

"You stay here," whispered Boculy, who wanted to reconnoitre.

I agreed but wanted him to take a gun bearer with him. He shook his head. It was pretty brave of him. He never would have stopped a stampede. He would have been crushed to a pulp in two minutes if the animals had started his way.

Hardly had he gone ten feet when I saw him jump into the air with a smothered exclamation. I ran ahead a few steps. Right there beside him was the largest cobra I had ever seen. It was at least ten feet long and as big around as my arm; it was lying flat, not coiled, as one would expect. Its head was about two feet from the ground and its neck was spread out larger than my hand in anger.

Boculy retreated trembling all over. He could hardly speak he was so terrified. He was not scared of elephants but snakes always frightened him. Hoping to chase the reptile off the trail he carefully selected a stick from some dead brush beside the trail and threw it at the creature. The snake struck viciously at the piece just as it fell. We could have shot it, but did not want to disturb the elephants.

While this snake interlude was going on we made so much noise that we waked up the herd. The first thing we knew twenty or thirty of the big animals were screaming and snorting around us, crashing over trees, banging into one another, and creating a general pandemonium. Luckily for us they decided to run away. Two minutes later they had disappeared. Once more the jungle silence had descended. Even the cobra vanished.

This is one of the thrills of our work. It is never possible to tell whether the death with which we are surrounded in many forms is going to descend upon us or going to evaporate. Whichever happens it usually happens quickly and without much warning.

We found the trees full of baboons on our way home. I could not photograph them on account of the places they rested, always under a shady branch. Anyway they seemed pretty insignificant after elephants. They were all chattering and squabbling with each other, which meant they were happy and undisturbed.

After supper Osa and I strolled a few hundred feet from camp into the forest. The trees went way up into the skies, so high that the stars seem to nestle in their topmost branches. Every tree was straight as an arrow, with not a limb until almost at the top.

We walked along back to camp slowly without speaking. We were still thinking about the

elephants. Suddenly there was a terrific uproar in
the tops of the trees. A large bunch of baboons
had settled down for sleep. When they saw us,
they came shinning down the trees all around us.
Some of them slid down in such a rush that their
hands and feet must have been blistered. Sometimes six or seven would collide with one or another,
landing on each other's heads and shoulders, all
falling to the ground in a bunch. Others would
jump when they got near the ground, landing with a
grunt and a thud.

Babies fell off their mothers' shoulders. Others
were abandoned in the tree-tops, screaming and
crying and trying to scramble down. I saw one
mother, torn between curiosity and love of her baby,
glance first at us and then back into the tree-tops.
Finally her mother instinct got control and she
clambered back to her little one while we went along
to bed.

It might be interesting to record just what boys
accompany us each day on these jaunts. Here is our
usual list:

2 Camera bearers.
1 Tripod bearer, carrying two tripods.
1 Boy with the lens case.
1 Boy with the Press Graflex and tripod.
1 Boy with a case of loaded film magazines.
1 Boy with two cases of loaded plate holders.

A SLEEPY OLD ELEPHANT IN THE NORTHERN GAME RESERVE.

The Northern Game Reserve is close to the Abyssinian border. The weight of this elephant's tusks is about eighty pounds each, totaling one hundred and sixty pounds. As ivory brings about five dollars a pound weight in Nairobi, it can be understood why elephant hunting is popular.

BEFORE THE CHARGE.

There were fifteen elephants in this sleepy herd, although only one—a big female—was aware of us. We had our cameras set up on a trail and she came up three times ready to charge. Each time she lost her nerve and turned back with the herd drowsily following. It was a peculiar situation, for she was as alert and as angry as an elephant ever gets, while the rest of the herd was not aware of us until the lady charged on the fourth attempt and we had to shoot her—just as my film ran out. The others then stampeded away.

1 Boy with 4 x 5 Graflex and tripod.
1 Boy with case of odds and ends: ray filters, tools, oil, medicine case, extra spools.
1 Boy carrying lunch.
My gun bearer.
Osa's gun bearer.
Boculy and Bukhari.

Each boy knows his duty. All withdraw to a shady spot behind me while I am taking pictures, but each one is on the alert, ready to bring me whatever case he has been carrying. Each case is numbered and I call for it by number. The gun bearers crawl along the ground to get beside me in the event of danger.

As time went on we had a chance to study individual elephants and their behaviors. One of the most entertaining sights was always a female elephant with her baby. An elephant is weirdly proportioned in every direction, from its curling trunk to its silly little tail. When its features are reduced to miniature, as in the young animal, few more comical sights can be seen. True, there are young elephants in the zoo. But there the mothers need show little of the assiduous care we so often see in Africa.

I remember coming on a number of elephants one broiling hot summer day on the plains. One mother was accompanied by a baby that could have been but a few days old. The little one was suffering pitifully from the heat. It whined and wobbled and persistently refused to keep pace with the older animals. Finally the mother lost all patience with it. She knew just what to do. Pausing at a nearby waterhole she proceeded to give her toto regular jungle heat treatment. First she butted the little fellow off his balance and held him down with her big forefoot while he lay squawking. Then she sucked up a trunkful of mud and squirted it all over the suffering infant's body. Despite his protests she repeated this performance again and again until her baby must have been greatly recovered.

Surely elephant parents are the most tolerant in the world. I have seen them submit to all kinds of inconvenience on the trail from skylarking young-sters. But when the adult's patience becomes exhausted, chastisement with trunk or butting head is always sure to follow.

A young elephant holds to its mother's tail with its trunk when passing through long grass just as a child holds its mother's hand. When she pauses in the shade of a tree it goes to nursing just like any calf. Strange to say, an elephant's udder is at the front end of her body.

One day about noon we were almost on the edge of the desert we came upon three full-grown females, one half-grown male, and one little toto, the smallest

elephant I have ever seen; it could not have been
more than a week old. Osa nearly cried out, she
wanted it so badly; but she controlled herself, though
I could see that she was trembling with eagerness and
delight in the way she has when anything strikes her
as particularly beautiful or cunning.

They had not caught either sight or scent of us and
I placed my cameras, grinding away, as they went
through their maneuvers. First the four older
ones would walk ahead, then pause to wait for the
little toto, which would come running up like a
clumsy little pup, back off, then charge under his
mother for its dinner. Then it would lie down
lazily and the others would considerately wait until
it had had its nap out or they thought it had had
enough. Then the three would start off, the mother
nudging it gently until the little one would at last get
up and join the others. All then journeyed slowly
on until they reached a mud puddle. Here they lay
down, rolled and threw mud over each other, the baby
having as good a time as any of them.

While they were playing I had left my first station
and crept up to a bush behind them. But the
quick-witted mother, catching the move, turned to
the baby, which had trotted off towards me, threw
her trunk around it and held it tight for a few seconds,
at last giving it a little slap with her trunk, as much
as to say. "Here, cut that out. Don't you go running

away or you'll get into trouble!" This done, off they started again, in little stages, always waiting for the baby, who was forever playing, to come up; and so they disappeared in the forest.

Not long after we saw another small herd; but as we were in the open and in plain view, one of the mothers in the case discovered us. A moment she stood uncertainly not knowing what to do; but at last decided to return into the forest, first turning just before she disappeared and looking at us as if daring us to follow. A moment later we heard her scream, with an accompanying little tin whistle effect from her baby. For several minutes after they disappeared we could hear the screaming of the big females and a flock of babies trying out their new trumpets.

From time to time we had adventures with single elephants. In a way these were more interesting because they gave us a different angle on elephant character. With a big herd around one had to keep so much on the outlook that detailed observation was difficult.

One morning we fell in with a big bull wandering about by himself. We sighted him some distance away feeding amongst some young trees. Through the glasses we could see him bending the thin trunks down and nibbling the tender leaves.

Skirting the spot widely we put the wind right so it

would blow from him to us and not reveal our presence. An elephant supposedly has poor eyesight, although I have a suspicion this theory may be one to his natural indifference to other living beings, acquired through centuries of practical immunity from attack. At any rate, it is sometimes possible to get right up to him if one watches the wind. The trouble is that on a hot calm day little breezes whirl about so capriciously one is betrayed no matter how much trouble is taken. We hustled the camera boys and gun bearers along until we were within about fifty yards of the big fellow. Our safari column was well away and there seemed to be no other game present except the elephant. This was providential because it meant that he would likely go on about his business long enough for us to make a good film and plenty of stills.

Luck played into our hands. Gradually our jumbo wandered closer and closer. Osa was bursting with excitement. The natives could scarcely restrain their exclamations of delight as well as of apprehension. The high point came when he was little more than twenty feet away, literally towering above us. He chose a tree that was too strong for him to break with his trunk, so he put his brains to work as well as his muscles. Pulling the sapling down as far as it would go with his trunk, he held it with his tusks while he reached up and got a new hold. He repeated this twice.   Finally the tree snapped and he wrestled the whole upper part down to the ground. Slowly he went to work among the leafy branches, selecting the tender young shoots and buds.   It was superb!

When he had eaten all he wanted he walked around the tree and came directly toward us.   As there was no use taking any more movies, I had Osa pick up her rifle while I used the still camera.   About the third snap the elephant suddenly saw us.   He stopped so abruptly that his huge bulk swayed in our direction.

Now he did the things an elephant does when he is startled.   His great fan ears went out as if to catch the slightest whisper of sound.   His long trunk projected forward, waving sinuously in the air like a black snake while he sniffed away for some telltale odor that would reveal the identify of the strange intruders on his meal.

We did not move.   Osa stood braced and ready to shoot if the fellow charged.   The boys bravely held their ground.   I "shot" another still or two in order to record the fine picture of elephantine curiosity before me.

Now we witnessed a characteristic of the dignity of these animals.   A rhino would at once have charged angrily or have galloped off in cowardly fashion.   One of the cat family, a lion or a leopard, would have lashed itself into a fury.   A giraffe or zebra would have changed its mind half a dozen times, advancing and retreating until it dashed off in a panic of fright. Not so the elephant.

After a long smell and the best look its little beady eyes could take, the elephant backed a pace or two, then slowly turned and walked deliberately away. He was not angry; neither was he afraid. He had probably never been shot at in his life. Had he decided we were enemies he would have charged; we knew this by sad experience. We were very thankful that he didn't, as we were right out in the open with no cover or refuge.

Not long after this we fell in with another elephant that took our presence in a much more animated fashion. He was feeding like the first one. But the background was different, and he behaved as if he were really wide awake. So I determined to film him. I managed to get the cameras set up in a wide open space before he saw us. As Osa was tired out after a hard morning she stayed back on the top of a high rock from which she could watch the surrounding country. In a few minutes the elephant started coming in our direction. At a distance of about thirty yards he backed off to the tree from which he had been eating. But he was too nervous to continue his meal.

Once more he came to investigate us, walking in comical little goose steps as though ready to charge or to run at the slightest provocation. About fifty feet away he began circling to get our wind. His short black tail waved stiffly in the air and his trunk was out. Finally he got a sniff of us. He didn't like it. He began to lash his tail and stamp the ground. His trunk swung angrily to and fro. But he couldn't for the life of him make up his mind to charge. When about forty feet from us he ran back a few yards, then whirled and came at us again. He had his head held high in the peculiar way elephants have when they are angry. He did this four times.

All the while I was getting priceless films. Finally the old warrior lost his nerve. I think it was the fact that we did not retreat which undermined his courage as much as anything. He just turned around all of a sudden and ran as fast as he could for the nearest cover.

When we got back we found that Osa had been crying. Through the glasses she had seen another elephant throwing water over itself from a waterhole. He then came in the direction where we were making pictures. He saw us photographing the other elephant and seemed about ready to charge. Osa was terrified that he would get us before we saw him.

Not all our encounters ended so tamely. One day, very early in our African experiences, Boculy came running into camp. I could tell he was excited because of the way his hands moved around. He

kept lifting them and letting them fall and then grip-
ping his fingers. He was saying things in short jerks.

"Big elephants," he exclaimed. "All together.
Very quiet."

By that we knew the elephants were feeding and
not looking for trouble.

I called to Osa to get her rifle. In five minutes
our gun bearers were under way with pieces slung
on their shoulders. The camera boys were swinging
up their heavy loads.

In fifteen minutes we were up to the herd. The
animals were out in the open. If we had posed
them they couldn't have been better placed for a
picture. There were three big cows and two bulls.
Two younger ones wandered around, bumping up
against the legs of their elders and grunting funny
little high pitched grunts. One of the bulls was a
fine tusker. His gleaming ivory showed milk white
in the sun.

This time Osa took the crank while I went forward
as "movie director" to start action among the
animals. I was afraid for her to go forward. There
was no cover in case the beasts charged.

She cranked away for all she was worth while I
walked gingerly toward the herd. The first thing I
knew the big bull saw me. He raised his trunk and
spread out his ears, shifting his feet about angrily.
He snorted. Then with a furious grunt he charged.

I ran. Sometimes we got our picture under such circumstances and then stopped the elephants by yelling and waving our hands. This time I was too close and the elephant gaining too fast. I swung about and tried to dodge. It was the only thing I could do to save my life. But my strategy was futile. The bull came right on for me. Like sheep, the other seven elephants tore after him. To my surprise there were about a dozen more behind these seven which we hadn't seen. Elephants seemed everywhere and they were all headed for us.

Osa was scared stiff but she kept turning the crank. She knew she was getting a superb picture and there was nothing she could do about me yet.

By the time I reached the camera the elephants were only a few feet behind. Osa's gun bearer had been at her elbow every instant. Now with one quick motion she took her rifle from him and fired. It was an easy shot so far as a target went. Her target was as big as a barn. But it took a lot of nerve to stand there and shoot under the circumstances—shoot and hit a fatal spot.

Her shot didn't kill the elephant at once but it diverted him from his murderous course. He nearly knocked the camera down when he passed it. He fell a little further on. The herd hesitated for a moment. Then all turned and ran.

Another time we were forced to shoot because the

boys became excited. We had reached the camp after a hard day when the guides reported that a herd of elephants had kept just ahead of them all day. While we were eating Boculy went out to reconnoitre. Ten minutes later he rushed back with word that the herd was right near camp. Tired as we were, we went right after them. It was ideal photographic country because the bushes were small and far apart.

In fifteen minutes we saw the elephants, fifteen of them, feeding about and taking things easy. The light was fine. I set up the cameras, intending to get closer after I was all ready. But when the elephants started our way I decided to remain where I was. First came a young female, and behind her in single file the others, mostly half grown, and one toto about nine months old.

The leading animal saw us when she was about sixty yards away. She stopped and the others crowded behind her. I think she was the only one that really saw us. She stuck out her ears and came on several times in little goose steps; then backed away and worked herself into a rage the way an elephant usually does under such circumstances. She lashed her trunk and stamped her feet. The others seemed unconcerned through this performance, showing only slight signs of curiosity as to what it was all about.

Then all at once I could see her gather herself just

like a runner. This time she charged. At the same moment the film ran out of my magazine and I started to load again, knowing that Boculy or Bukhari would stop the beast in time. Meanwhile Osa was making stills. But when the elephant got within fifty yards she grabbed her gun. Then, unexpectedly, at a distance of twenty yards Boculy shot, then Bukhari. Boculy shot again, each time knocking the charging elephant to her knees. On the last round I yelled for them to stop shooting. Then I read the riot act to the two boys because they should have waited until the other white man with us, Mr. Saunderson, had decided to shoot. It is one of the worst crimes a black can commit in Africa, to shoot before his Bwana. Had they been alone with me it would have been all right. Happily, the female ran away with the herd and Saunderson assured me that her only wound was a flesh one on her trunk.

Osa had her own private experiences with the cameras and elephants. Without telling me, one day, she took what she thought was my best Graflex and walked over to the Old Lady Waterhole, two miles from our camp. The camera was carried in a black leather case swung over the shoulder of her black boy. A bull elephant, two females, and a little toto were having a great time here, throwing water all over themselves, shower-fashion, with their trunks; and the mother was giving a bath to her baby. After the infant was bathed and dried in the sun, he made for his mother's udder, and nursed away, both mother and child as happy as you please. The old bull walked bravely about, raising his trunk and stripping the buds from the trees. Now and then he uprooted a sapling, much as a boy leaps over a gate from sheer joy of living or to show his strength. It was altogether a happy family party.

Often on the plains the light is not favorable, for the heat waves, which amateurs mistake for light, prevent clarity. But here conditions were excellent. Osa, too, had taken pains to get to the windward of the elephants, not always an easy task where the breezes curl and eddy through the dongas. Now she asked her boy to hand over the camera, her eye still on the happy group, determined to surprise me with an unusual picture. But when she looked down at the black leather case which she supposed to be a camera, she discovered to her horror that she had brought our medicine case along instead of the Graflex. She spent two hours that evening telling me what a beautiful picture she might have had.

One thing I often noticed about elephants was what seemed to be a sort of mental telepathy that went on between them. I have seen this sort of thing so many times that I have wondered if it were possible there could be some sort of wireless operation that goes on. The elephants have very stiff hairs in their ears and in their nostrils. These could readily be used as antennæ to catch emanations that the human being is quite unconscious of.

On many occasions I have seen an elephant, separated by perhaps several hundred yards from the rest of the herd, seemingly warn his comrades of a danger he himself has discovered. It almost seemed that he sent some mental signal to the others, for they would suddenly become restless and alarmed, even though I am sure they could not see the lone elephant nor discover the danger for themselves.

One night Osa and I were in our blind down in the mimosa near the lake with the moon shining between the drifting clouds, waiting to see what would turn up. About 11.30 P.M. Osa nudged me. Four hundred yards to the left of us appeared a long file of elephants. They walked to a spot not far from our flashlight apparatus and stopped there for about five minutes with their long trunks up in the air waving about as if for a scent. Then one elephant left the crowd and walked very slowly down towards the water. He would go about fifteen feet, then stop and wave his trunk about; then go on a bit more. We could see him so plainly that he gave us the impression of being distinctly puzzled, feeling there was something wrong, but not sure what it was.

Then this investigator walked back to the rest of

the herd and for about fifteen minutes they all held a sort of conference. Not a sound, mind you; just a standing quietly around as if whispering together. I know they could not have seen the apparatus, for I had it perfectly concealed. It wasn't the wind either; our position was such that it would not have been possible for the wind to have blown from us to them. Nevertheless some sense told this elephant that something was wrong, but what he wasn't sure. Moreover, he was not going to advise his friends to take a chance. Finally, they all quietly made their way to the water by a route that took them around the cameras. After a good drink they melted soundlessly into the forest and we got no picture.

As time went on the elephants got bolder whenever their food dried up in the forest. Every night we would see them and they would trumpet through the evening hours, as they crashed through the boma, until they came alongside our house and caught the human scent.

One old lady developed the habit of breaking into our garden. The drought now had dried everything up but the sweet potatoes, which like camels can go a long time without water.

This elephant was particularly orderly and systematic, choosing a space of about ten feet square and eating ten feet square of sweet potatoes, then going away without disturbing any of the surrounding plants. In this care she differed from almost every wild animal I have known.

We noticed that she entered the boma, the thorns of which did not seem to make much impression on her leathern hide, at a hole she made alongside a great yellowwood tree. There we set up our wires and cameras and we had just gone to bed when we heard the boom and ran out taking our rifles with us. In the woods nearby we heard a terrific thrashing and found that the elephant had carted away about four square yards of our boma, from which she was trying to free herself.

So thrilled were we at the prospect of another good elephant picture that we took our plates to the laboratory as we were, in our pajamas, and there developed them. They came out wonderfully sharp and clear, showing two elephants apparently; in reality only one, for we had caught the sweet potato thief going and coming.

This lady, we thought, would not visit us again, but next night we heard the boom and found that this crazy elephant had rushed away with four more square yards of our fence. Again we developed the films in our pajamas, getting a thrill out of it, I think, that no slaughtering hunter knows.

We felt sure that now we had seen the last of her. Still, elephants are of one track minds; they keep on coming in spite of all obstacles. And again, this

"Sweet Potatoes" —A Nightly Visitor.

We called this lady "Sweet Potatoes" for she liked them better than anything in our garden. She would walk carefully down the paths between rows of lettuce and radishes and tomatoes, and when she came to the sweet potatoes she would stand in one spot and eat a space of about ten feet square. She ate both potatoes and vines, and always turned up the next night to eat another space. This picture shows her entering the garden.

THE ADVANTAGES OF BEING A PERFECT LADY.

Here is a picture of the same lady as in the preceding picture—taken the next night as she left the garden, after coming in at another place. Because she was never destructive we never molested her. In fact, we actually planted sweet potatoes for her to eat to her heart's content.

third evening, we heard a breaking of branches on the edge of the forest, and a general thrashing around and found the same matriarch grazing contentedly, pulling down her branches and nipping off the shoots. No big booms of flashlights were going to disturb her; and to show that she was not afraid, she walked through the hole in the boma which she had just made and went along the row of houses, where the boys slept, like a runaway elephant going up a town street; and quietly proceeded to strip off one of the thatchings as a final gesture of independence. It must have been startling for the boys to wake up and see the roofs being slowly lifted off above their heads and in a moment we heard a succession of cries and the straw huts disgorged frightened black figures that ran, tripped, and tumbled on all fours all up and down the narrow path.

This, of course, was trying even though it enabled us to study the ways of elephants. And indeed hers were not the usual ways of elephants. Every part of the garden was reeking with the scent of the boys, which would not have disturbed the elephants of Siam and India, who are trained in captivity to draw great trunks of teakwood trees and to plow, but almost always send their wild brothers of Africa crashing through the trees. The boys solved the problem by saying simply that that *"tembo"* was crazy.

We gradually became so accustomed to elephants that we felt far less fear of them than we should have. A curious experience some time later showed that it is not safe in Africa ever to be off guard.

We started out one morning for a donga several miles away and on the trail noticed a grass fire a considerable distance from us. About 10 A.M. Osa spotted four elephants in the donga below us, one young bull and three females. I got to work with my camera and inside of thirty minutes had used every lens, from the shortest focus to the longest. By this time the elephants had decided to graze. They left the trees and came out into the opening, slowly gathering grass and throwing it over them, now and then pulling up a young tree.

Suddenly we were made aware of the unexpected approach of the fire by a sudden roar of flames. Apparently the conflagration had almost died out at a small donga beyond the elephants; but on crossing it had come to dry grass as high as our heads. Now it swept down on us with the speed of a train. We were standing on a small peninsula of land where the donga took a turn. Before we knew it we found ourselves entirely cut off; in every direction the grass was on fire, already scorching us with its heat. There was but one thing to do, and that was to go over the little cliff nearby and take our chances with the elephants.

I am still wondering how we escaped broken necks and cameras. We all went over the top together, falling and scrambling down the cliff towards the elephants. The latter whirled about and stood with trunks out and ears up. At this moment they, too, got the roar and scent of the fire. They stuck their tails into the air and dashed for the far side of the donga, while we followed at best speed. When we emerged the elephants had disappeared.

Boculy told us one day that elephants do not care about their rears; these are almost impervious to bullets and even spears. But he could not explain how it was that flies and tick birds annoyed the great animals.

Then Osa wanted to know how long they lived; but all Boculy could say was, "Many year"—he could not count far enough. But I informed her that some of the books had recorded a hundred and seventy-five years as a very old age for an elephant; and, barring spear and rifle catastrophes, most lived considerably past the century mark.

I have often heard people boast about killing an elephant. We were both sorry we had to kill one. Our thrill came in a fine film and a narrow shave.

Years of this sort of work have of course given me a pretty close insight into elephant character. My views have changed since as a boy I watched circus elephants on parade. In fact they are still changing as I live more and more with the unspoiled animals.

I have come to look upon an elephant as the dignified old gentleman of the wilderness. Often he is of great age; and his size prevents his plunging about the way lighter animals do. Yet he is not sluggish the way other elderly beasts come to be; it is only fair to cite the rhino as an example of an undignified creature despite his size.

Certainly the elephant is no fool. He attends to his own business and lets other creatures severely alone. He leads a quiet family life. And he does not prey on the land or lives of other species.

That the Indian elephant is easily tamed is no reflection upon the elephant's character in general. He is not weak willed. Rather does he possess a kind of native philosophy deeply planted in his heart. Quicker than the cats and more thoroughly than the cattle does he perceive the futility of resisting captivity imposed by man. So he goes about his tasks or his tricks calmly and efficiently, and probably enjoys life little less than when he was free.

I do not take any too seriously stories about an elephant's vindictiveness. I think most intelligent lower animals remember a human being who has wronged them. Dogs do. Also there are vicious members of the elephant family just as of most other kinds of animals. A vicious dog or horse is equally on the lookout for trouble, though their smaller size makes less impression on their keepers when trouble comes.

I like elephants and I admire them. And I believe the normal pachyderm elephant is a kind, conservative animal that knows his place in life and is wholly content to keep it.

CHAPTER VIII

ATTACKED BY RHINOS

NATURALLY there were some serious adventures with the wild animals we met. No circular letter had reached the game to say that we were not out to harm them. We were not aggressive, but we were bold. And in our constant intrusions we often took chances.

There were almost no tragedies, though we had many narrow escapes. There was the case of Rattray who was badly mauled by a leopard when helping Osa.

In view of what happened later, it was strange that about this time Saunderson, my young assistant, got word that two of his friends had been killed by a rhino. It seemed that a young lady was staying with friends near Nanyuki. She went out with a Meru boy armed with a .303 Army rifle. The pair came on a rhino which charged and killed her despite the fact that she bravely fired six shots into it.

About the same time a settler and his wife were returning from Meru in a Ford. They saw the same wounded rhino on the road. Unluckily the gun was lashed to the seat. While the wife was untying it her husband jumped out and tried to frighten the rhino away by yelling at it and waving his coat. But the animal charged and killed the man right before the poor woman's eyes.

Soon after this I came out of my tent one morning and saw three rhino coming towards camp. They were fighting and running at the same time. There was also a baby rhino along which kept whining as it tried to keep up with the older ones. It seemed tired and was no doubt frightened at the rumpus its choleric elders were kicking up. Then the whole crowd disappeared in some bushes.

After breakfast, Osa, Furber, Saunderson and myself went to the place where we had last seen the rhinos. Saunderson and Furber went into the bushes to look for tracks. All of a sudden I heard a scream. Then two shots, then more screams; then another shot and more screams.

Osa and I dashed over as fast as we could go and entered the bushes. Saunderson was stretched out on the ground with his clothing torn and a mass of blood. At first I thought he was dead. But we raised him up and found the rhino had got him in the legs. He was badly cut up on his upper right thigh where a horn had torn to the bone. We quickly carried him into camp where luckily the cook had plenty of hot water. I washed all the gashes and put permanganate on them.

When the injured man could talk he told me that he had nearly stepped on the old female. She came for him instantly. He got in two quick shots but they glazed off her horn and thick skull. She kept coming and knocked the gun out of his hands and gored him.

Saunderson died a few weeks later of pneumonia.

In one way or another we came to know a good deal about the rhinoceros. The distribution of this animal is rather general over East Africa. We found them both on the plains and in the forests. The latter species have a larger and more tapering horn. Possibly this is the result of the plains animals going to live in the wooded sections where use of their horn against trees is common.

It is interesting that the difference between the horns of the plains and forest rhinos is said now to be less marked than formerly. Probably the plains animals are taking to cover as a result of the advance of civilization.

We found young rhinos with their parents at all seasons of the year. The family sticks together until the young one is nearly as large as the adult. Percival tells me that the rhino's reputation for viciousness comes largely from the fact that he tends to doze during the day time. When man disturbs him he wakes up half frightened, half angry and full of resentment.

Warning of the approach of danger is given the rhino by the tick-birds that forever are roosting on top of his back. The birds fly up in alarm at the slightest provocation and the host comes to enough to find out whether it's worthwhile waking up. If the birds seem really frightened the rhino also becomes very much excited, and does not calm down until he is positive that everything is all right. The intelligent instincts of these guardians is noted from the fact that they do not seem to mind the presence of man when on domestic cattle; it is only on wild game like the rhino that they flutter away when the hunter approaches.

The next day after Saunderson's scrape we had another brush with rhino. At daybreak I was on a small hill with my camera watching a herd of buffalo in the grass below me. As Bukhari was ill my second headman was acting as chief. I told him to reconnoitre while I went back to camp. On the way I saw coming toward me full tilt one of the boys.

"Humadi killed by rhino!" he gasped out.

With my heart jumping I ran after the fellow not knowing what horror I was about to see. He led me to Humadi, one of the porters, who was lying on the ground close to camp pretty badly, though not fatally smashed up. I carried him into the camp where he was roundly jeered by his fellow tribesmen. It seems that he had walked head on into the young rhino whose mother had gored Saunderson. The baby was so scared it charged the black, knocked him down and stamped on him.

Next morning it rained in small showers and I thought the day would be a washout altogether. But Boculy said that we should find rhino before noon; and we did. It rained like the devil for fifteen minutes, then the sun came blazing out in all its African glory.

Right ahead of us was a herd of twenty-seven giraffe. A few minutes later Boculy pointed out a rhino across a deep valley. I had to take my glass to see it. But before I could focus on it the native announced there was a "toto" or baby rhino with it. I wish I had eyesight like that. It took us an hour to get to the animals, with the bad going and our heavy cameras. And when we got there the big mother had gone to sleep under a wide bush. We could not see the toto so we sat down to wait for her to wake up.

About three o'clock the old woman came to and let her baby have dinner. We did not dare move or she would have seen us. A mother rhino and baby are a dangerous proposition. We were right out in the open. In a short time she decided to ramble on and started toward us. She was about the size of a coal truck, and roughly the same color.

The instant she got our wind she snorted and ducked

her big horned head. Boculy and Bukhari stood by with their guns ready in case she came for us. There was no assurance that a rifle shot would stop the beast had she taken it into her head to charge our way. But the two black lads stood bravely by waiting our call for their assistance.

Just when the rhino was about to charge we set about shouting and waving our arms and were able to head her off before we had to shoot. I might add that I think this sort of thing usually meant that the animals were only half-hearted in their attack. For when either lion, rhino or elephant really took it into its head to vent its anger on us we usually had to climb a tree or shoot.

In angry dignity the mother rhino went down through some rocks slowly enough for her baby to follow. She snorted away at the comical little fellow from time to time because it waddled too slowly to suit her. We heaved a sigh of relief when she passed out of sight.

Another time we had been watching a rhino go up and around the cliffs near the lake with a sureness that seemed impossible in such lumbering brutes, and a little later a big rhino mother with a little toto came down to the pool. This baby too was not over a week old, and was still unsteady on its feet but frisky as a kitten. It ran under its mother's belly, as she drank, butted her playfully, then ran away for a few steps and then back again. But every time she tried to get it to drink it would shy off.

Fascinated, we were watching it, and commenting to each other in whispers about the timidity of rhino young, which often stick by their mothers until as big as they. And I had arisen from the ferns and was cranking my camera—as the little one ran off from the pool, then, frightened by some leaf or bird, ran back again—when Osa gave me a nudge. I turned quicker than a shot and there, coming for me, was a big buck rhino, his two horns straight in a line with the camera —and me. Osa already had her rifle—they were always across our laps, by our bedside, somewhere near at hand—at her shoulder, the .405 Winchester; and I called to her to try and turn him with a shot rather than shoot to kill, for I was making a good film of him and I thought this might be one of his everlasting false charges. Evidently Osa didn't think so, for as he came within thirty feet, she shot for the brain and he fell; the bullet, we later found, lodging right by his horn.

It is easy to imagine my anxiety when, after such incidents as these, Osa disappeared one day. She had ridden out a little way from camp on a mule; with her was one of the gun-bearers who reported that somehow or other he had got separated from her. My fury at the man's being so casual was tempered when I saw how really frightened he was.

At once I organized a search party. Not only were there rhinos in the vicinity, but leopards and other carnivorous beasts. If Osa was hurt and unable to defend herself there was no telling what ghastly fate might be hers.

Of course it was not unusual for her to be treed by a wild animal. I knew she would climb out of harm's way rather than shoot game unnecessarily. But I gathered from the man who had seen her last that there were no climbable trees within several miles of the desert trail they were on when he lost her.

From a rocky elevation I searched the plain with my glasses. To my intense relief I suddenly saw Osa sitting alone on the ground at least a mile from me. As I looked she rose slowly and started to walk in faltering steps our way. We rushed out to meet her.

"The mule shied at a snake," she explained. "I fell off, and lost consciousness. I think I must have struck my head on a stone."

It was a good lesson in the danger of going alone through such country.

I think we found the rhinos mostly feeding on the unpleasant thornbush. Sometimes they would turn up under a solitary tree on the plains which they had selected for their daytime rest. Despite their choleric temperaments we found them regular in their habits, and tending to stay in the same neighborhood. From this we learned not to pitch our tents on a rhino trail as the animals were as likely as not to come trotting carelessly along down wind and blunder squarely into camp. During the day the rhinoceros does not drink much, putting in more time dozing or fighting. About 4 P.M. he feels the need of a drink after the torrid heat and begins to wander toward his neighborhood waterhole, feeding as he goes. After a drink he will play by wallowing around in the mud, or pick a choice fight with some worthy antagonist. He spends a good deal of the night wandering restlessly about, grunting and squealing in marked contrast to his silence during the day.

It is probable that few animals suffer so much from native hunters as does the rhino.

I remember one exciting evening when Osa and her guide, Bukhari, climbed a ten foot rock some distance back of our camp. I wanted to get some photographs of rhinos as they went down to the waterhole for a drink. We agreed on signals in advance. One whistle, repeated at intervals, meant a rhino was coming in front of us; two that he came from the left; and three from the right. If Osa saw one coming up behind us she was to give four blasts.

With one other man I lay down in the sand about twelve feet from the flashlight lamps which were set up by the trail to the water.

About ten o'clock Osa gave one whistle. It was

pretty dark and the fact that a big brute weighing several tons was headed in our direction was not altogether reassuring. I later asked Osa how she felt. "I was too excited to feel," she said.

In a few minutes we could see the monster coming right down the path for us. Osa had considerable responsibility on her hands at the moment. For not only did she know her husband was in line with the animal, but she sighted another at almost the same moment. Furthermore she had no way of telling whether or not we had heard her first whistle.

The heavy thud of footsteps soon revealed the whereabouts of the oncoming rhino. When he was within a few feet I set off the flash. He went galloping back in Osa's direction.

In a few minutes another rhino came along. More whistling and a flashlight. This went on until about midnight. Osa kept busy whistling until she stopped in despair. There were so many rhinos coming and going that she could not keep track of them. Finally we had to throw stones at them to keep them away from us. As for poor Osa she was held a prisoner until after 2 A.M. when she found it safe to join us in camp for a well-deserved night's rest.

Once at one of our waterholes we dined well in the evening, for Osa took her Ithaca twenty, a shot gun with which she accomplished marvels, and came back with two dozen sand grouse. Contented and full, we slept well, only to be awakened about midnight by that chorus of snorts which always betrays the rhino. There, just beyond our makeshift boma, two rhinos were at it, snout to snout, quarreling over some fat-rumped dark leather-covered belle who stood watching the proceedings. Like the baboons in our forest, who are constantly threatening and pursuing each other, but rarely coming to actual fisticuffs, they did not give us a run for our money. They kept circling about, made lumbering sorties at each other; stood, heads lowered, tails in air, snorting away, and pawing the ground like enraged bulls; then seemed to kiss and make up. Possibly the presence of unseen white men acted on their subconscious minds, taking the fight out of them; or else they were staging a sham battle for our entertainment as we lay there in the moonlight. At any rate, that was the end of the affair. The peculiar thing about their exit was that they left the trail and gave our camouflaged blinds a wide berth though the wind was all right. On the way they met two other rhinos coming in, conversed with them a moment, snout to snout, and then the two newcomers repeated the same maneuver, leaving the trail so as to avoid our concealed cameras. Evidently they had been warned by the others that there was a queer looking structure down there by the water.

Next morning I went out alone with the boys as

A Rhino that Claimed the Right of Way.

Enlargement from movie film. This rhino was on his way to water, but as we were set up on his trail, he could not help noticing us and charged full tilt.

Stopped by Osa's Bullet.

This is the same rhino, the picture being made at the instant Osa shot him at a distance of thirteen feet from the camera.

A FOREST RHINO ON THE PLAINS OUTSIDE LAKE PARADISE.

He has just been informed by the flight of the tick birds that there is danger about, and he is whirling around trying to get the scent. A minute later he got our wind and charged, but we went up trees and he passed under us and went off into the forest.

Osa felt she should fish; she was very conscientious about this as she said we needed fish for every camp in which we could get them. We left camp about the same time and walked about a mile together before she branched down to the river, riding on her mule. Ndundu and Butoto were with her. She had perhaps gone a quarter of a mile when I saw her and the boys running, a rhino after them full tilt. Ndundu fired twice but missed. Butoto scrambled to the top of a big ant hill.

Although I was afoot I started off at a run to the rescue, my boys following. But of course I was too far away to avert disaster. Anyway the mule was so terrified that the rhino had no chance to catch him. The chief danger lay in the chance that Osa might lose her seat and fall off. About this time Osa saw me coming and the rhino apparently heard us. It wheeled and disappeared in the long grass near the river.

No wonder Osa hated rhino. She was always having encounters of this sort with them. When she came up to me she was so angry that she wanted me to go right back with her and shoot the beast; but in a few moments she cooled off and laughed about it.

Here I discovered a small matter that might have led to serious consequences besides the fight it led to between Osa and Ndundu. It seemed that he had placed only four cartridges in the gun that morning

instead of the regular charge of five. Osa wanted me
to discharge the boy, but Ndundu was nowhere to be
found. He did not show up that night. Next morning I found him waiting for me outside my tent.
He was so sorry he actually cried, so of course Osa
forgave him and all was bright again.

Some of the intensity of desire with which we
searched for rhinos at this time was gradually communicated to our boys. One day, while we were out
near one of the mountain waterholes, two of them
went to the pool for water. On their return they
reported they had seen rhino which that particular
morning we very much wanted.

"Did you see them?" I asked.

"Yes, Bwana Piccer."

"Good rhino?"

"Yes, Bwana, very fine!"

So off to the waterhole we went. There had been
no rhino there for twenty-four hours, so Bukhari
declared, and we knew enough now of the signs of
the trail to realize that he was right.

"Why in the devil," I said to the luckless boys,
"did you say there were rhino? Why did you lie
to me?"

"But, Bwana, there were tracks."

"They were old and you did not tell me
that."

"Yes, Bwana, that is so. We knew that; but two

rhino had been there. Had we been there yesterday, there would have been rhino."

"I suppose they were beautiful rhino then."

"Ah, Bwana, fine rhino, the biggest you ever saw," so expostulated the rascals, though the game may have been quite ordinary; then,—"Do not be angry with us. You want good rhino and we only want to help you see good rhino."

With such childlike good nature and naïve philosophy we had constantly to contend and it all added much to the countless other difficulties of the expedition. However, it afforded some amusement, on calmer reflection, and relieved the tedium of some of our journeys. And often I tried to sound the boys out, to delve into the dark chambers of the brains of these people, who have been sunbaked for centuries into indolence and stupidity and who have been rendered hopeless by constant oppression from Northern tribes and too often from the white traders, to say nothing of generations of slave hunters before them. It is not all their fault.

At times I think the rhino work got a bit on my nerves. The creatures themselves were stupid. The heat was often terrific. And the boys, like children, had their temperamental ups and downs in the most unexpected fashion.

I recall one morning in rhino country when I especially instructed the boys to remain together as they followed us with our gear. They tended to straggle along and string out all over the landscape until our chances for rhino became practically nil. About 9 A.M. we sighted a rhino ahead in some volcanic slag. We halted the safari and taking the camera boys told the others to remain behind until we called.

Now we located the rhino again and got very close to him by going carefully. I set up my camera and was patiently waiting for him behind a bush. Suddenly he snorted and ran. On looking for the cause I discovered my safari going around a hill a quarter of a mile ahead. The boys had disobeyed and thought they would go on. As a result they gave the rhino their scent and my two precious hours went for naught.

This was a bad day altogether. About eleven we came upon another rhino and this time you may be sure the boys remained behind. Osa and I with the cameras managed to get up close enough for a few scenes, when the sun went under a cloud and the party was off for the moment. Then a pest of flies descended on us and bit our flesh until we nearly went insane. Also dust and heat waves made photography almost impossible.

The last straw came when the rhino found we were after him. There was only one small thorn tree near the camera, up which I put Osa when the beast began to graze in our direction. Suddenly he got our scent and came for us in short goose-like jumps. Then when his little near-sighted eyes focussed on our party he stopped and pawed up the ground as if to say, "Come on, I dare you to fight." Then he charged. It was funny to see nine boys and myself trying to climb that miserable little thorn tree after Osa when there certainly wasn't room for more than three of us. Fortunately Mr. Rhino decided that he had taught us a lesson. He circled the tree with his little tail stuck straight out and then dashed off.

A somewhat appropriate accident happened just when we were working back from our base and were passing through some of the plains country inhabited by the irritable old rhino. We had left several cars at a place called Merille. Millions of bees had colonized our camera boxes built into the bodies of the machines. We tried every way we could think of to drive the insects out but they went right back. I tied mosquito nets over myself and went in with sticks and scraped the boxes clean of bees. The angry creatures swarmed about me until I could not see. Then they got inside the netting. In a frenzy I ran away tearing off the netting as I went. Osa and the boys came to my assistance, as a result of which everybody got stung. Boculy had one eye shut; both my ears were swelled to twice their normal size; and the bees were back in the cars.

Then I tried tying the netting about me and driving one of the cars up and down the road as fast as I could go with one hand, while I scraped out the bees with the other. This worked. But the minute I stopped the bees came back. Finally we simply had to burn them out, which played hob with the cars but left us 400 lbs. of beautiful honey.

CHAPTER IX

THE CREATURE GOD FORGOT

WITHOUT the giraffe in daytime and the noisy hyena at night Africa would not be Africa. The giraffe is one of the first animals you see when you arrive and one of the last to peer at your fading dusty trail when you leave.

One day near noon, near the upper edge of the Kaisoot Desert we came suddenly on a pitiful sight; a dying giraffe, neck broken and twisted almost under him. Up the poor creature's back were a series of four sets of lacerations, each set grouped within a radius of about six inches.

"Lions!" cried Osa.

Boculy, our black elephant guide, shrugged his broad shoulders and grunted one word: "*Simba*," the native name for the king of beasts.

The giraffe's great soft brown eyes gazed pleadingly up into mine for a moment, then glazed. Sadly I reconstructed the scene that must have taken place not twenty minutes before our arrival.

The waterhole at hand nearby told where the victim had been drinking when set upon by its assassin. A few yards away was a clump of young trees, the tops of which were green and tender. This was another clue to its fate. For after it browsed among the thin African foliage it turned to drink. As it poised awkwardly over the water a tawny blur behind a nearby rise on the rolling plain crept slowly forward.

In my mind's eye I could see the swish of the big cat's tail as it slunk along with that dreadful running crouch at which the lion and leopard are so skilled. To be sure, from time to time the wary giraffe glanced nervously about. But to fill its long sharp mouth it must plunge nearly its whole nose into the scummy water, fatally shortening its vision. At these instants the lion darted forward, each time gaining ten yards or so on its prey. When a hundred yards away all cover ceased. The instinct of the giraffe had arranged for that. Then the charge: a galloping dash so swift that the horrified giraffe sensed but a yellowish light over its shoulder.

Probably at ten feet the wet-jawed lion sprang. He landed with claws bunched on the rump of the doomed giraffe. Heart pounding with dread the giraffe set off at the best speed nature had given it. But this speed was as a child's tottering run compared with the hurtling death behind. Nor did the lion cease to run now that he was aboard. He literally galloped right on up the creature's back.

Hence the groups of lacerations where his claws had dug deep for a foot-hold.

Astride the shoulders of the giraffe the lion balanced for a second. Then with one powerful upward sweep he caught the despairing creature's long neck with the claws of one massive paw and apparently hove it down until the vertebræ cracked.

Such is murder in the wild spaces of the earth.

If there lives a more defenseless animal than the giraffe I should like to know about it. To be sure a giraffe can run faster than an earthworm; it can kick harder with its front feet than a caterpillar; and it can see better than a mole that is blind. But the earthworm has its hole; the caterpillar can roll up and play dead under a leaf; and the mole lives hidden from his enemies.

The giraffe abides on the open plains amidst lions and leopards. To everyone of these carnivores its flesh is an appetizing delicacy. The giraffe is grotesquely conspicuous at all times. Its neck is ridiculously out of proportion to its body, which in turn is foreshortened to a stumpy and unbalanced lump. Its legs are so stiff and ill-formed that it must drink by spreading them apart until it takes a violent effort to spring to attention in case of danger. Its teetering gallop is thrown out of balance by the weight of its long neck. It has no claws or teeth for combat. It can make no sound to frighten its enemy or warn its comrades.

Surely the pervading Wisdom of the Universe slipped a cog when the wretched giraffe was allowed to wander into the African den of lions among which it leads its guileless life. It cannot fight, run, cry out nor hide well enough to escape its bloodthirsty enemies.

I think it was Conrad that once said the best way to deal with injustice was to ignore it. This is what the giraffe does. He accepts the injustice of his fate with a dignity and gentleness that is worthy of the best traditions of a gentleman.

The family life of the giraffe is exemplary. We became so accustomed to the rowdies and grouches of the jungle that it was a distinct pleasure to fall in with giraffes and watch their bland goings and comings among the other animals. Never did they dash about kicking and snapping the way the zebras did; or snort and quarrel as is common with the rhino amongst his kind.

From time to time Osa and I came unexpectedly upon a mother giraffe and her gangling baby. The latter, like all its kind, was always consumed with curiosity. The sight of us two-legged animals was something entirely new. That we might represent danger seemed not to occur to it.

As the little fellow craned his long neck and trotted

a few steps in our direction the mother would become almost frantic. Having no vocal chords she could make no sound of warning; and unequipped with paws she could not maul her infant the way a bear would have done. Her only recourse was a sort of panicky trotting round and round the young animal, punctuated by a series of nudges that made little or no impression on the little one's burning desire to find out what we were and why.

This made a splendid picture of mother love. The adult gave every sign of terror. She knew we were not like the grazing animals to which she was used. Probably our movements were nearest to those of the beasts of prey that she knew would find a tasty morsel in the tender haunches of her child. Yet she would not desert it. And not until the silly little creature consented to trot away with his adoring but terror-stricken mother would she leave our vicinity.

One strange phenomenon we often saw among the giraffes was a half-grown female followed about by several babies. Osa was sure that this was some sort of "nurse maid" arrangement. She used to report to me of a night, "Martin, I saw a herd of giraffes today with two nurses and five children." Probably the truth of the matter is that the mothers are killed by lions while defending their young. The infant manages to escape during the struggle and rejoins the herd. But since the other adults are already taken up with their own young the orphans must band together for mutual protection.

Of course we never were able to make a study of the animals until we saw them in an undisturbed state at or near a waterhole. One scorching day I sat reading in my blind. The animals outside were logy with the awful heat. A miasma of white dust filled the air, kicked up by the thousands of hoofs milling about me. This dust prevented good photography; but I hoped the air would clear later in the day.

Suddenly I heard something picking away at the roof of my shelter on the side away from the waterhole. "Ah-ha," I thought, "that baboon again." One had been annoying me for some time. "Now I'll get him."

Quietly laying down my book, I crept to the S-shaped passage through which we entered and stuck my head out, ready to club the knave who had the temerity to tamper with my edifice. To my surprise there was not an animal in sight, save a herd of wildebeest and zebra some distance away. I craned my neck about, still hoping that I might ambush the intruder. In my hand I gripped a light stick with which I hoped to get in at least one blow of chastisement.

Deciding that the baboon had heard me coming out and had run away, I was about to return to my time-killing task when I heard a rustle over my head. I glanced out and found myself looking into the familiar brown eyes of a towering giraffe right above me. Apparently he had found some succulent buds among the fresh thorn branches that had been laid over the roof of my retreat. He was startled, yes. But there was no move of vicious defense as there would have been on the part of every other animal out there on the plain. Clearly he was sorry to have intruded. I could almost see him bow slightly and say in a low voice, "Really, I didn't know this was your place. I beg your pardon, sir." Quietly he moved away, gentle, voiceless and innocent of any desire to work harm to any other living being in the land.

A giraffe's water system seems to be built like that of a camel. In the south country natives and guides have told me that the giraffe never drinks. For years I never saw one do so. Yet no one has ever seen the gerenuk or the dik-dik drink. They get their moisture from certain roots, cactus-like bushes, trees that have a milky substance in them and from the tender young buds of trees.

One day in the Southern Game Preserve Blayney Percival and I were talking about this curious trait of the giraffe. Neither of us was sure what the animal's drinking habits were; though we both knew that it must imbibe moisture somehow or other in order to live.

Suddenly Percival seized my arm. "Look!" he whispered. Right below us on the edge of a little pool stood a full-grown giraffe. After a long scrutiny of the country around, it approached the water very slowly and waited as if listening. There was no cover for a lion to hide behind, except for the little knoll on which we perched; and the land about was as flat as a billiard table. For long minutes it seemed as if the giraffe were only going to have a look at the water. It craned its silly neck this way and that; it cocked its eye at the pool, which must have been very tempting to its parched tongue. But it did not drink. Nor did we move. I think we both were anxious to see what the animal would do.

Finally it began slowly to spread its four feet. Despite its long neck it could not lean over far enough to reach the surface of the water. It had to lower its whole body by dropping the center of gravity in the same way one lowers a moving picture camera by spreading the legs of the tripod. Once it assumed this awkward position the giraffe seemed to realize that the sooner it drank the safer it was. Only by a sort of hop and rear could it possibly assume its position for running again. His long neck swung down. Into the water it plunged its slender tapering nose and drank for what seemed an hour to the pleased pair of men who were spying on it.

I found the same thing later at my waterhole

blinds.   The giraffe always took longer than any of the other animals to come down to the water.   Time and again it would get almost to the edge and then be startled by some stamping giraffe or other beast. It was not afraid of the other grazing animals.   I once saw a dozen giraffe pass within ten feet of a grazing rhinoceros and pay absolutely no attention to him.   But they no doubt know their shortcomings; and are prepared to flee if any other animal is attacked by the meat-eaters who are always hovering about.

If the waterhole is among reeds or grass, or up a small ravine, or in any other kind of country that affords cover to lurking enemies the giraffe will not drink.   More than once I have seen a herd of them that I know could not have been to water for days, avoid a hole in the most sweltering heat just because it did not offer a safe visit to a creature so awkward. Even out in the open I have seen a single giraffe take over two hours covering the last few feet between itself and the water.

Men cannot really be counted among the enemies of the giraffe.   Sportsmen seldom kill them.   It is possible to secure a hunting license that permits it. But there is little of the triumph for the big game campaigner that goes with conquering an infuriated lion, buffalo, elephant or other truly hostile denizen of the plain or jungle.   Once the hunter gets within rifle shot of the giraffe there is no trick to kill it. There is no danger and no dodging. Indeed its curiosity puts him at an even bigger disadvantage than its helplessness. For it will stand and watch a safari until the travellers are out of sight. It will watch as long as it dares when the hunter approaches. And even when it runs it will not go far because its curiosity soon gets the better of its fear.

Sometimes Boer settlers kill giraffes for their animal's hide, which is the second only to that of the elephant and the rhinoceros for thickness and toughness. By slicing a cylinder of the hide around and around the Boer fashions a long durable whip which, when properly cured, makes an ideal article for driving his oxen which he hitches in teams running above twenty animals. The skin also makes excellent harness and boots. But the British government recognizes the likelihood that the giraffe will soon become extinct and protects them assiduously against commercial exploitation.

Natives rarely kill the giraffe, though the meat is considered very tasty by them. Their greatest desire for a dead giraffe rises from their superstition that the hairs out of a giraffe's tail are fine medicine against the onslaught of evil spirits. They braid this hair, which is black and wiry, into attractive bracelets and necklaces which they wear night and day.

GIRAFFE ON THE SERENGETI PLAINS IN TANGANYIKA.

Someone has started the rumor that giraffe are becoming extinct. Instead, the truth is that they are on the increase. In good plains country one will often see hundreds in a day—perhaps a thousand in different herds. I have personally seen eighty-two in one herd. I venture to say that in the whole of Africa there are more than a million giraffe.

A MOTHER WITH ONE OF THE HARDEST JOBS IN THE WORLD.

A mother and baby giraffe on the Serengeti plains of Tanganyika. This mother has the most peculiar markings we ever saw on a giraffe—the markings being leaf designs. The difference between these and the usual markings is readily noted. A giraffe baby is always full of curiosity, but having no vocal cords, the mother can't call it from danger, so she must watch it helplessly until it has investigated what the peculiar people are. Then the mother gets up her nerve and comes bravely back to stand beside her youngster.

Whenever in our travels we come upon a giraffe that has been killed by lions our natives make a rush for the carcass in hopes that the jackals and vultures have left the precious tail intact.   I must add that such a find is not as valuable as we used to think. Our guide Boculy later confided to me that the hairs from a dead animal have lost much of their effectiveness in keeping away the devil.

A settler was once talking to me about his superstition and laughing over the native's insistence that the hairs from the tail of a live giraffe make good medicine.   He related the following incident:

"I remember seeing twenty giraffe bogged in a mud swamp.   We weren't after the poor devils. Somehow they got ahead of us and seemed to think we were chasing them.   Before we knew it they had galloped straight into a morass that we knew was badly mired after recent rains.   I should have thought the animals' instinct would have kept them out.   But I suppose they were so frightened they lost their heads.

"We went up and tried to do something to help them.   But our presence only made them struggle deeper and deeper.   We went away hoping that when we got out of sight they would manage to escape from the clinging mud that dripped their slender legs.   Otherwise the group would either die of starvation or of fright.

"Next day we came back to see what had happened. The giraffes were still there, *but every one had had its tail cut off*. That meant the natives had been in after them for the miracle-working hair. Not one animal was harmed."

Whether they finally escaped is a question. I certainly hope they did.

Indirectly man caused the death of a lot of giraffe when the Uganda railway was first built. The common giraffe, which is sometimes twenty-three feet from the crown of its head to the sole of its hoof, continued to wander about its preserve as its ancestors had for countless ages. Naturally when a hungry lion hopped into the midst of a herd of the tall animals they fled in all directions. As a result the railway engineers used to find a dead giraffe every week or so lying near the track with a broken neck. Running madly through the darkness the animals had collided with the telegraph lines with fatal results. For years an average of over 50 giraffe a year committed suicide this way.

It is practically impossible to tame a giraffe. I know of one that was lassoed and died of fright before it could be got into a cage. Half an hour after the rope was around its neck it collapsed. I once saw a baby giraffe that belonged to a settler, but it did not seem at all contented with its surroundings. It was nervous, and anæmic and gave every sign of

longing for the wild plains on which it had first seen
the light of day.   Most giraffes that are captured
die of a broken heart before they become used to
captivity.   On the other hand giraffes in confinement
give very little idea of those we see in the wild state.
I suppose only those that are semi-morons can endure
living without their freedom; as a result almost none
of the wild animal's personality survives.

Despite this the giraffe is one of the most sought
after animals for menagerie or zoo.   Justly so, too;
for it is one of the strangest creatures that survives
from prehistoric times.   It is the tallest animal man
knows.   Its curious spots vary from beast to beast;
once I saw one with distinct leaf markings down
in Tanganyika; and a native killed an albino in the
Lorian swamp some years ago.   Some have nearly
black markings, others with their pattern so dim as
to be nearly invisible.   In a herd it is interesting to
note that few have the same shade of coloring, all
ranging from dark roan to light yellow.

Classed by color and markings there are two kinds
of giraffes in East Africa.   On the lower edge of British
East they are blotched with dark markings on a light
ground.   But when we get towards Abyssinia we find
their designs "reticulated"; that is to say, they are
mostly dark with a network or reticulation of white
lines placed in a large pattern thereupon.

In this connection it is interesting to note that the

history of man's knowledge of the giraffe compares favorably with the records of sea serpents and the like. For many centuries the accounts of this animal put it in the class with fabulous monsters. Travellers caught glimpses of its great height and grotesque proportions and at once put it in the class with satyrs, sphinxes and unicorns.

It is recorded that the first giraffe ever seen amid civilized surroundings was exhibited in Rome in the time of Julius Cæsar. So great was the impression of the strange beast upon a very superstitious populace that other specimens were brought in whenever they could be got. The animals came in through the Egyptian desert and across the Mediterranean. But few withstood the hardships of such a journey. In those days the giraffe was known as the Camelopardalis (because it impressed the naturalists as a sort of combination between a camel and a leopard), which name stuck as camelopard until recent years when the more simple name began to be generally used.

Before 1827 no giraffe had come to Europe since the end of the 15th century. In this year a pair were sent as a peace offering by the Pasha of Egypt to the courts of England and of France. It is not on record what the Pasha thought the monarchs to whom the animals were addressed would do with these strange gifts. But doubtless he made an impression with this display of his imagination. Further, reports of the species had been so exaggerated that much excitement was caused throughout Europe by the passage of the animals. It is commonly believed that the average giraffe was "so huge that a man on horseback could pass uprighte under him." And that he fed on the leaves of the highest trees.

The next shipment north of giraffes was not until 1836. This comprised four animals and was an outstanding event in the natural history of that day. The quartette was led through the streets of the city of London by attendants especially trained for the task. Nubians in Abyssinian costume lodged the animals in their quarters in Regent's Park. Besides the guiding natives a whole retinue of servants brought up the entourage. Accounts of the performance are staidly humorous in dealing with those citizens who unexpectedly sighted the great beasts through eyes dimmed by recent dissipation.

It is curious that of all the African animals there are fewer anecdotes and adventures extant about the giraffe than about any other denizen of that wild country. No doubt this fact is as good a tribute as any to the giraffe's virtue in neither meddling in another's business nor in loving combat the way so many of the animals seem to.

Some tribes of African natives used to claim that a giraffe often sleeps with its head high in the crotch of a tree in order that it may keep a good lookout for trouble. While it dozes it continually shoots out its long slender tongue that is narrow and curved so that a pencil could scarcely be inserted in it.

Not long ago a giraffe killing was witnessed from the windows of one of the trains on the railway running from Mombasa to Nairobi. Apparently the noise of the train hastened the attack of the lions and gave the giraffe some sense of the danger she was in. At any rate they seemed to rush in with less assurance than usual. The giraffe at once put up the best defense of her child she could by kicking out right and left with her forefeet, but not abandoning it. The train stopped to give the passengers a chance to watch the spectacle of this cruel and one-sided combat.

Undaunted by the roars of the lions an American newspaper reporter at this point sprang from his coach and rushed out, unstrapping his camera as he ran stumbling over the dry hard ground. Cries of warning by the train crew, who knew only too well the peril in which the tenderfoot was placing himself, did not deter him. As so often happens in dealing with wild beasts the very boldness of the man unnerved the lions. At the photographer's approach they made off leaving their wounded victim to escape in another direction. But she did not run far; for her little fellow stood there where she had left him, helpless with a leg she herself had broken in her wild efforts to keep off the lions.

The natives tell of a certain comradeship that occasionally seems to exist between elephants and giraffes. There are certainly traits of similarity between the two animals. Both are inclined to live and let live. Both have dignity and decency in their relations among themselves. Both make excellent parents. And both are grotesque survivors of a prehistoric age of mammals.

Schillings, the African traveller and explorer, relates how he fell in with a big male giraffe consorting regularly with a pair of elephants for mutual friendship and protection. Probably the giraffe could see further and better than the elephants; and the elephants in their turn prevented attack by the giraffe's worst enemy, the lion.

Another curious belief among some of the natives is that giraffes talk to one another by means of their tails. It is true that when the bull of a giraffe herd sights an enemy he at once emerges from the tree foliage amongst which he may have been feeding and begins whisking his long bushy tail about at a great rate. When the giraffe is suspicious there is also a great switching of his tail.

CHAPTER X

A DESERT NINCOMPOOP

"BOOM-BOOM-BOOM-M-M!" My friend, on safari for the first time, threw a startled look out into the black African night. Beyond the narrow cylinder of our camp-fire's glare, the green eyes of big preying cats shone at intervals. A heavy body rustled through the bush. A hyena laughed hysterically on the rise behind us and was answered by another cackle of his species in a little donga near by.

"Boom-boom-boom-m-m!"

My friend reached out and gripped my arm. For a moment I thought the night had got him. It does, you know, when you are not used to Africa; when you realize that half a dozen lions are out there a stone's throw from where you are sitting, their long tails slashing in murderous irritation at man's fire which they dare not face; that a shadowy leopard is slinking in your tent's short shadow for a closer look; that an ill-tempered rhino may be at that very moment on his way to investigate the human intruders.

172

Yes, night on the African veldt can easily get the newcomer.

"Boom-boom-boom-m-m!"

Of a sudden I was conscious of my friend's real perturbation. His hand on my arm gripped tighter as he pointed with the other in the direction of the sound to which every African traveller becomes so accustomed; the only other continued night noise besides the demented laughing of hyenas.

I laughed. The African dweller always laughs when he answers this particular question.

"Ostriches," I explained. "Only ostriches. Their booming is the most common, the most carrying, the most senseless of all animal speech, yes, even more so than that of the crazy hyenas."

"Boom-boom-boom-m-m!" again like some gigantic bullfrog of the desert.

Less is known and more is misunderstood, I think, about this huge bird—that isn't a bird—than about almost any other animal in the world.

There is a pathetic vanity about an ostrich that other animals seem to understand far better than man does. An ostrich doesn't walk, he struts; he doesn't scratch, he preens; he doesn't look from side to side, he cocks his head with a silly archness quite in keeping with his whole dude-like personality.

I remember sitting in my blind one morning at a waterhole waiting for the game to give me the film I wanted. There were zebra, gazelle, wildebeeste and wart hogs about in thousands. Unfortunately, the weather was scorching hot; and since it had not rained for days, a powdery dust rose under the nervous hoofs of the animals and filled the air with mist-like clouds that made photographic work impossible.

My chief amusement came from watching the ostriches as they stalked down from time to time to drink. They came individually. Each strode slowly through the herds, his head pompously high and his long legs thrust out affectedly at each step. Though he looked neither to the right nor left the quadrupeds made way for him. I watched carefully to see if perchance there would be a collision at any time. But there wasn't. However, I have long since been convinced that other animals are afraid of the ostrich's terrible kicking power.

Having reached the water the ostrich settled itself in its tracks and glanced haughtily about. If it was a male, he usually swallowed a time or two. Had he worn cuffs I am sure he would have shot them, probably taking a silk handkerchief out of his breast pocket to wipe his beak before the first sip. Were it a female, she rose slightly on her toes and fluttered her wings before settling herself to the serious task of quenching her thirst. Somehow this performance conjured up the vision of a lady twitching her shoulders and coyly pushing up the edge of her veil.

The actual drinking consisted of two motions: a shovel-like dip of the beak into the pool and an upraising of neck and head while the water ran down the long neck. This was repeated several times, with a deal more of the comical hitching and gesturing between mouthfuls. As I have said before, it is this drinking act that has given rise to the tradition that the ostrich hides its head in the sand when pursued by man.

The ostrich chiefly flourishes in Southern Africa. I am told that Xenophon in his *Anabasis* mentions having seen it in the southwestern desert tracts of Asia. In East and South Africa the big birds inhabit every waste extensive enough to give the arid solitude an ostrich seems to love.

The wild ostrich is disappearing rapidly on account of man. To be sure, it is preyed upon by the carnivores, but not seriously as compared with the native and settler who trap it for domestication. Before 1860 the ostrich was a wild bird. In 1862 half a dozen chicks were caught in Cape Colony for the purpose of experimenting with them as domestic fowl. It was realized that the feathers were valuable; and the eggs were of such size as to promise returns, provided they were as edible as reported. The first hatching was in 1864. To the vast satisfaction of the pioneer the chicks proved a success; in fact, with careful feeding and housing, they soon became more healthy than their parents.

Today there are nearly 20,000 highly bred birds in South Africa alone. These produce 85 per cent of the world's total supply of feathers. The other 15 per cent comes from North Africa, Australia and California, each producing about 5 per cent. California birds are said by experts to give feathers nearest in quality and size to those of South Africa. Diet is probably the determining factor in the feather quality of our home state.

In early days the best white feathers sold at seventeen shillings a pound. Now pure white feathers bring as high as fifteen to twenty-five pounds a pound. Price varies with fashion on one side and the supply on the other. But since the altogether unrelated ups and downs of both do not at all coincide, the ostrich raiser can never be quite sure where he stands.

Wing and tail feathers are clipped when the bird is seven months old, but the finest plumes come from birds two to thirty-five years old. Each wing gives about thirty white feathers, weighing around half a pound. Double that quantity of tail feathers come from a bird, but these are considered second in quality. Light and dark feathers from the female are not so much in demand as the fine pure white

COMMON ZEBRA AT A CHOBE WATERHOLE.

It is an interesting fact that no two zebra are marked alike. There seems to be as great a variety of zebra markings as there is of finger-prints. Study this picture and you will see what I mean.

LORDS OF THE WATERHOLE.

For some strange reason, other animals usually make way when ostriches drink. It takes these ungainly birds so long to fill their bills that they appear to be burying their heads in the mud or sand of the waterhole. This probably has given rise to the old legend.

ones from the male. From both sexes hundreds of small grey and black fancy feathers are cut to thin the heavy coat the birds grow when healthy. These are sold for dusters.

I must confess that most of my interesting experiences have been with the wild birds. I find them far more engrossing, though less beautiful, than the fat domesticated fowl, which are usually logy with overfeeding.

Osa and I are always glad to get back to a mess of ostrich eggs. We like them best scrambled, though they can be prepared in any style. Each egg weighs about three and a half pounds, and, from a culinary point of view, is equal to about three dozen hen eggs. It takes forty minutes to soft-boil an ostrich egg and at least four hours really to hard-boil it; once done it will keep for weeks.

I remember an afternoon when company came suddenly. Osa told one of the ladies she guessed she'd make a cake for dinner.

She disappeared for five minutes and came back with the remark, "Well, that's that."

"You don't mean to say you've made a cake in that time!" exclaimed the guest.

Osa beckoned the doubter to follow her. "One egg, one cup of flour, and a pinch of salt," she laughed, "and you have a cake."

There on the table was the huge shell of one ostrich

egg with a gallon flour bucket by its side. The native cook had just slid the cake into our hot-stone oven. It was just a case of putting the whole operation on a gigantic scale, with cup and egg nearly forty times their conventional size.

Another time when we were held up at night by storm we stopped for shelter and a bite. I had not yet been in Africa long enough to learn the ways of the country. After we were seated in the dim rays of a single oil lamp that flickered in the drafty room, our host removed a trapdoor from a corner of the floor and lifted up what appeared to be a large white rock. Taking his hammer from the shelf, he went out and could be heard chopping away at something. Presently he returned and laid a shining hard-boiled ostrich egg on a plate. He sliced the egg and served it on green leaves, with salt and pepper and hard ship's biscuit. Rarely had anything tasted so good.

The proper number of eggs under a setting ostrich is approximately sixteen. I suspect the ostrich never counts them but depends on the way they feel under her; for she will try a nestful for a while and kick out one at a time until those left feel right.

As a matter of fact, the nest life of an ostrich is just about as ridiculous as a good deal of the rest of its life. Both sexes set. The male, being of a darker hue, takes the night watches. I suppose he is quite invisible to prowling animals in the dark. The grey hen, almost exactly matching the dry grey desert, takes over the job during the day.

There is some doubt whether the ostrich depends on the heat of the sun to help the hatching process. I have frequently run across nests of eggs with no bird around. But never have I done this when the sun was at its full tropical force. Surely the scorching heat of an African midday would penetrate even the thick shell of an ostrich egg.

In breeding season one cock goes about with four or five hens. Most of the time he pretends to be utterly indifferent to the ladies in his harem; but he eyes them, none the less, while they mince and preen and otherwise cast their net for his majesty.

If another cock, especially a young one, arrives on the scene and makes any advances towards the hens, there is a terrific rumpus right away. The king-pin prances about and makes jerky threatening motions with his powerful foreleg that tell the intruder in no uncertain language to beat it. The youngster never fights, but prances away in skittish fashion, pretending that he didn't mean anything serious at all.

After some days the hens begin to work on the love nest.

There is only one nest for the whole family, which is both inconvenient and impractical. But such is ostrich fashion, and ostrich fashion is just as foolish as that of the human being. The site of the nest is out in the open, as far as possible from any sort of cover. Obviously, the ostrich wants to be able to sit on its nest and catch first sight of any approaching enemy. The minute a stranger appears on the horizon the ostrich is up and off on a wandering course that cleverly misleads the jackal or hyena that might be searching for its eggs.

The nest is simply a shallow pit scraped out of the sand and gravel by the feet of birds. The sand is banked up slightly on the outer edges to form a low wall against which the eggs can rest without rolling out. This is one of the few purely practical and intelligent things of which the ostrich is ever guilty. When about a dozen eggs have been laid the cock decides to get down to serious business and begins to roost on the collection. The hens, always anxious to please, straightway follow suit, taking turns as convenient.

So far, so good. The trouble is that the hens don't associate the size of the nest with their contributions to it. As a result, they go right on merrily laying. After there are about twenty eggs the nest is full. Even then the energetic hens don't stop. Soon the male begins to be annoyed by the mounting cargo of his nest. Playing no favorites, he doesn't hesitate to kick out enough eggs to make himself comfortable for the night. Just as likely as not one of the zealous hens will come along next day

and roll some of the extra eggs back in again.   This
foolish performance goes on for several days and
sometimes until there are more than forty eggs in all.

I have seen nests surrounded by a dozen broken
shells from which the contents have been emptied.
It is said that when the young begin to be hatched
the parent breaks open some of the remaining eggs to
feed the chicks which cannot stand the rough food of
the desert.   But I am inclined to doubt this.   Probably the broken shells are only sad signs of the
hungry hyenas who have slipped in while the cock
and hens are away at the water hole and had a meal
at the expense of their labors.

Natives steal eggs by locating the nest and waiting
until the birds are off.   Sometimes they will throw
rocks on the hen left behind on guard, driving her far
enough away to make it safe to approach.   It is
against the law in South and British East Africa to
rob an ostrich nest, but the blacks do so whenever
they are out of sight of authority.

Probably the hyena is the greatest egg thief of all.
So much of a scoundrel is this fellow that he breaks
more eggs than he can eat.   Such is his practice
in his other hunting; indeed, I have seen him ham-
string goats, one after another, when there was no
chance in the world of his ever feeding on them.
Small felines, such as the gennet, civet and wild cats,
also enjoy an ostrich egg as a change of diet.   Herds

of running game, zebra, antelopes and wildebeests, break a good many when stampeding over the nest.

Theoretically the ostrich will not come back to its nest once it is disturbed. But natives and old-time African hunters know how to do this skillfully so that the ostrich does not seem to mind. The important point is not to touch the eggs that are to be left.

Our common domesticated fowl usually sets on twelve eggs and takes twenty-one days for the hatching. The ostrich often completes its setting on as high as twenty-six eggs, from which the chicks emerge after forty-two days.

The little ones are at a terrible disadvantage at first. Their legs are so long and weak, their necks so slender and willowy, that they are more like intoxicated creatures than like infant fowl. They reel and stagger about aimlessly for some days, an easy prey to the first carnivorous animal that happens along.

Meanwhile, alas, the parents revert to their former vanity. The cock, wings spread and neck curved backward, struts about with a grand air of "How is that for an old man?" while the hens are mincing around him, rising on their toes and settling back, or teetering sidewise with their bills cocked at a deprecating angle, all the while seeming to say to one another: "There, I told you so!"

While father and mothers and chicks are still all together in the early stages of this period of parental pride the young can still rely on some protection if the cock notices a jackal or hyena advancing. At such times the ostrich is very ferocious and will boldly charge the beast who threatens the safety of the chicks. Sometimes, as a ruse, he even pretends to be lame. But even this gesture of defense is part of the whole prideful personality of the big bird; for when the danger has passed he does not return for anxious investigation of his offspring to see if they are still safe and sound, but struts up and down with an air of braggadocio to advertise the splendid courage he has just shown.

With such a streak of moral weakness running through ostrich parenthood, it is not unexpected to find the chicks drifting away altogether from their fathers and mothers. Often have I seen them out on the veldt wandering around in forlorn groups with every appearance of never having known true motherly love. Once Osa and I came on a bunch of twelve big ostriches accompanied by at least a hundred poor little ostriches. The big birds looked just like a bevy of rich tourists pretending they didn't notice the ragamuffins that were following them about. Our hearts went out to the little fellows, who seemed utterly miserable and full of doubt as to what to do next.

The full-grown ostrich sometimes weighs more than three hundred pounds and is as much as nine feet high. His most marked characteristic is the fact that he has only two toes—the third and fourth —on each foot. In South America there is another large bird—the rhea—which is also called an ostrich. This bird can be distinguished from the true ostrich by its having three toes instead of two. According to the biologists the original ostrich had five toes. However, the modern bird can probably run faster with the two it has now than could his ancestors with five.

Arabian legend has it that the ostrich is the result of union between a camel and a dodo bird! Certainly it inherited some of the worst characteristics of both. Its awkward shape, the uselessness of its wings, its seeming lack of pleasure in life, all indicate that it is one of Nature's errors.

The one offensive weapon at the command of the ostrich is its foot. The terrific downward stroke of its huge toe driven by a muscular thigh the thickness of a leg of mutton is easily the equal of the kick of a full-grown horse. A blow from it will break a rib or the backbone of any ordinary animal. In addition to the force of the blow, the sharp claw can tear skin and flesh like a military saber.

I remember once when a native was standing in front of an ostrich that was to be caught for plucking.

GOING FOR A FREE RIDE.

Two of our pets—a young lion cub and a half grown baboon. They were quite good friends. They slept together, and whenever the cub decided to move the baboon would hop on his back for a free ride.

AN IMPROMPTU BATH ON THE NORTHERN FRONTIER.

Our bathrooms often were dug in the sand river beds. Water seeped in and made excellent bathtubs,

Suddenly the ostrich was frightened by a man coming up behind. He plunged forward and struck at the black, ripping him completely open. It is for this reason that when the bird is plucked the plucker usually leans on him from behind, since no ostrich can kick to the rear.

The philosophy of the ostrich seems to be built on a too-proud-to-fight basis, as I have never seen them attack one another. But no doubt beasts of prey are wary of that vicious downward blow, as I have never seen signs of an ostrich having been killed by another animal.

I think one of the most remarkable ostrich adventures of which I have ever heard happened in Boston. One night a drunken man reeled into a dark shed of the Zoo where an ostrich was kept. The huge bird rose to defend itself when the man staggered toward the corner where it had been sleeping. By sheerest accident the man's hands came into contact with the creature's long neck before it had a chance to strike the usual murderous blow with its foot. Luckily, the man hung on. Ensued a terrific struggle to the death of the ostrich.

African natives capture and pluck ostriches with a gentleness that is altogether unexpected. They take advantage of the fact that the bird probably loses all defiance when its head is covered. The native fashions a cone of bark the inside of which he smears with a sticky gum of a resinous tree. The cone is then filled with a particularly succulent shrub of which the ostrich is very fond. When the bird has eaten down to the gummy lining the cone sticks on its head completely blinding it.

Now the native can approach the ostrich with impunity, though he must remain in rear of the bird so as to be clear if it kicks. The ostrich farmer resorts to the same general method, except that his paddock man employs a long bamboo rod with an iron crook at its end to pull the bird's head in. A small black cap, like a hangman's bonnet, is then fitted over beak and eyes and tied some inches down the wriggling neck. Though twenty men could not pull the feathers out or clip them before the bird is thus blinded, he is docile as a kitten once he cannot see. I should add in passing that there is not the slightest pain connected with the clipping of an ostrich. No doubt it is a relief to the bird to be rid of his hot coating.

The natives have no utilitarian use for the feathers. They bedeck their shields and spears with plumes very much as did the knights of mediæval times. In ceremonials, ostrich-feather ornaments play a considerable part in making the native and his trappings both colorful and impressive.

I don't think I should mind a tame lion or leopard or elephant. Even a tame zebra or buffalo can be made useful, if not ornamental. But an ostrich is the last creature in the world I should want about the house. In the first place the poor things are regular nesting places for incredible swarms of vermin. No doubt this misfortune accounts to a considerable extent for the constant and ridiculous jerking about of the average bird. Then the ostrich is the original sufferer from dandruff. I suppose it isn't real dandruff; but it looks like dandruff and it's just as offensive, with none of the human personality beneath it to hide the defect.

Once when my boys caught a young ostrich we gave it to a near-by government station. I passed by a year later and found the bird nearly full grown and very tame. But it finally got to be such a nuisance my friends had to give it away. They said it ate everything in sight that caught its eye—money, jewelry, glass, nails, small spoons, and so on.

I used to think that the things I heard about the appetite of an ostrich were exaggerated. Now I know they are not. The truth of it is that Nature impels the birds to gobble hard objects into their gullets to help grind the massed roughage that they eat. But, as in other things, the ostrich shows little signs of intelligence or restraint. I remember one bird was opened some time ago in a French Zoo and found to contain more than twenty pounds of iron, lead, copper, zinc, stone, wire and other articles quite useless so far as any nourishment was concerned.

The natives do not kill ostriches for food. Hunters say that in emergency the heart and liver of an ostrich make excellent eating. But for a regular diet I think they might be compared with the sea gull for which Jack London used to prescribe the following method of cooking:

"You put on a large kettle of water to boil. Pluck the gull carefully, making sure not to injure its feet or bill. When the water boils put the gull in, head down, and let simmer for fifteen minutes. Then throw the water away and repeat the process."

At this point in the story Jack used to pause impressively, raise an emphatic finger, and go on with every evidence of being very sincere:

"After having thrown away the third water," he would say, "you then throw away the pot and the gull, and have anything else in the world for supper. Nothing is worse to eat than a sea gull!"

Except, possibly an ostrich, I should like here to add.

I know of one case where a native had a tame ostrich that he taught to decoy other ostriches into reach of its master, who then captured the newcomers and stripped them of their plumes.

Both natives and naturalists have done some ostrich stalking by making an imitation bird which they enter and wear among other game. Natives fashion the body from long thin sticks covered with skin or cloth, dyed with mud to the color of the male bird. The legs of the man appear through the bottom as the legs of the ostrich. The neck is simply a real neck stuffed.

The wearer of this strange disguise crouches inside, holding the neck aloft with one hand. By pretending to graze about, peck at its wings and wander casually toward the waterhole, the man can approach within a few yards of other animals without creating the slightest commotion among them. It is curious that the ostrich can detect the subterfuge at a distance of more than a quarter of a mile, and at once becomes panicky at sight of this strange travesty on itself.

I have found that the motion-picture camera frightens an ostrich more than does a man, leading me to believe that the creatures are more observant than one would at first imagine. For the chief difference and novelty in the camera is that it has three legs, whereas in the ostrich's whole experience all creatures have either four or two.

CHAPTER XI

A CAMERAMAN'S TROUBLES

I MUCH doubt if any one who has not tried it has any conception of the difficulty connected with making wild animal pictures. To see all kinds of wild game roving about on the screen, most of the time seemingly unaware of the presence of the camera and the cameraman, often deludes the spectator into thinking that after all it is rather easy to photograph them.

Herein art and skill defeat themselves. The better an animal picture is made the less exciting it appears to be. The easiest thing to do is to shoot an animal with a high-powered rifle at a comfortable and safe distance, or to run it down with a motor car, picturing the process and its excitements. The hardest thing is to picture that same animal in a calm undisturbed state of nature. But that is the most important thing that the camera can attain.

I can well remember our first trip to Africa years ago. We arrived during the driest part of the dry season. All along the railway line from Mombasa to Nairobi, Osa and I saw thousands upon thousands of head of wild game—wildebeests, zebra, Tommies, Grants, ostrich, giraffe, wart hogs, kongoni and eland. We looked spellbound out of the window of our compartment. It was the most wonderful sight that we had ever seen, and we could hardly wait to get off of the train and start photographing. It looked so easy that we thought we might have our picture done in a few weeks—and have the world's greatest animal picture at that easily!

Two weeks after we had equipped our safari in Nairobi we were out on the Althi plains in our first camp. Then came disillusion. Game was everywhere, but the stubbornly suspicious animals would not let us get within camera range. For the first three weeks we snapped nothing but extremely long range scenes. Then to my sorrow, when I developed tests I found that the heat waves that dance in the distance had distorted and practically ruined the pictures.

Next we tried building blinds. We spent endless hours in them waiting for the game to come down to the waterholes within camera range. But there were too many waterholes and the whimsical, suspicious animals chose to drink elsewhere. They would not come near our blinds. After five weeks we gave up and went back to Nairobi. It was not going to be as easy as we thought.

Osa and I talked things over and decided on a new

strategy. We planned to make a long safari of nearly four hundred miles up to the arid districts in the north of British East Africa where there were far fewer waterholes. There we figured the game would be forced by thirst to come into the range of the cameras.

This long safari cost us much time and a great deal of money. When we arrived at last we found a new set of hampering facts. The nomadic natives with their herds were using what waterholes there were for their stock by day, and the game came down to drink at night. We safaried from one waterhole to another until at last we came to one that was unmolested by the natives. Again we spent weeks in blinds. We had to rebuild the blinds time and again, learning a bit at a time about how and where it should be done. It was more than four months after we landed in Africa before we had a single scene worth putting on the screen.

Problems of wild animal photography are many and complex. The camera makes certain demands. There must be fair light. Shadows must fall right else the picture will be flat and uninteresting. One must set up with such angles of view as to avoid bald skies and awkward compositions. The footing must be stable lest vibrations mar the picture. And that is only the beginning. The blind must be built to windward of the waterhole so that the human, or inhuman, scent of the camera man does not reach the animal on some wafting breeze. If possible, the blind should be slightly higher than the spot to be pictured because the scent, carried by the rising heat of the body, tends to go upward. Also the blind must be as perfect a bit of camouflage as possible. Wild animals have critical eyes. They do not admire a conspicuous blind. It offends their taste in land-scape and challenges their sense of discretion. They do not enjoy having their Africa tinkered with. They do not like the click of a camera either. They never get consciously confidential with a photographer. African animals have only two lines of action with reference to the camera. They either run from it or at it. Neither treatment is entirely satisfactory to the man behind the camera.

Most of the members of the numerous antelope family and the other grazing animals like the giraffe and zebra can be photographed from blinds. Also now and then one gets a chance at lions and leopards and other beasts of prey which follow the herbivorous animals to the waterholes. But there are animals in Africa which seldom or never drink—the gerenuk for instance. It is but the merest chance if such animals stray within the range of a waterhole blind. They must be stalked afoot by the cameraman. It is always a stern chase, which is notoriously a long chase—with usually nothing more to reward the effort than a handsome rear view of a vanishing animal with his tail waving goodbye as he goes over the hill.

The elephant presents a special set of problems to the camera hunter. Generally speaking, the elephant sleeps through the day and eats in the cool of the evening. We spent weary weeks following various small herds before we could catch them under light conditions which would permit the making of satisfactory pictures; even then we did not know enough of their habits to be able to get close to them. We tried to solve our elephant problems by employing Boculy, probably the greatest of all the black elephant trackers in Africa. But he often got us too close and we spent more time getting out of the way than we did making pictures.

We had been out on safaris for a little more than a year when Osa and I took stock of our results. We had spent a large share of the money appropriated for our expedition and felt we did not have enough animal pictures to make a satisfactory production. We decided we would simply have to take more chances and get closer to the animals, else the whole project would be a disastrous failure. So we threw caution to the winds and with our hearts in our mouths went back to work.

Now the fun started. We got pictures, all right, but every picture entailed a definite risk. I am half afraid now that a good many of our elephant pictures are too good. They make the elephant look hardly more dangerous than a slightly discontented cow. To get these pictures of the elephant in his own private home life meant the invasion of places where we were never supposed to be, in terms of any common sense. Often we had to run for our lives; and once we had to shoot our way out of a very bad mix-up. I suppose we had fifty close calls before we were satisfied with the pictorial results.

A great deal of the elephant work was in forest where pictorial problems are always the most difficult. The winds tend to blow from everywhere boxing the compass every few hours and carrying the scent of the hunter to all nervous animals. Further, the light is constantly changing with every change of position and directly under the trees there is very little light at all. Any trees or grass absorb a great deal of light; and one has to give about twice as much exposure in timber as on the open plains because there is no reflection from the dark trunks and leaves.

From about ten o'clock in the morning until three in the afternoon—when the light is the strongest—is not a satisfactory time for making pictures because with the sun nearly straight overhead, shadows obscure details in the animal and at the same time make the general scene flat. Moreover, this is the worst period of the day for the shimmering heat waves which are the bane of African photography.

Besides all these smaller handicaps there are only about seven months of the year when one may expect good pictorial conditions. This is through the dry season in the months following the two rainy periods. During the rains with water abundant everywhere the game scatters so widely that the animals are hard to find and travelling is difficult. There is a slight advantage in camera hunting the elephant during the rainy season when he leaves the forest for the plains, if one can only be on hand at the time; but it is almost impossible to follow him for considerable distances.

Photography from blinds is practical only in the dry season when one has the water to bring the thirsty animals into range. Blinds demand patience. They must be built and then left for a week or ten days before any attempt is made to use them so that the game will get used to considering them a natural and harmless part of the landscape. One must expect to waste a great deal of the effort made in blind work. Often have I built a series of blinds commanding a waterhole and then at the very time I started to use them the wind would shift against all calculations, and blow my scent toward the water.

I have one word of cheer to add to the lore of blind

photography. After some years of research I find that the taboo against smoking in the blinds is all a mistake. The animals seem to pay no attention to tobacco. I am not sure why. Perhaps it is because the animals are familiar with fires on the bush and veldt and the acrid smell of the smoke. But I am reluctant to libel the makers of my favorite cigars with any inference that their aroma resembles a jungle on fire. Anyway it is perfectly safe to take comfort in a smoke while waiting the coming of the suspicious animals.

The blind work on our last safari was the most difficult that we have ever experienced. This time, on top of all the natural difficulties, politics came to complicate affairs. A former head of the King's African Rifles on the Northern Frontier of British East decided he would solve all the problems of the territory by remarking the map. He moved the tribes about like checkers on a board, putting each tribal unit into a new and unfamiliar locality with new neighbors. The result was that none of the natives knew the regions that they were compelled to call home. This made them unhappy and restive. It also ruined waterhole photography in the district. The unsettled natives scattered about all the waterholes and built manyettas everywhere, driving the game away and making it wilder than ever.

On this last safari I managed to bribe several manyettas to move to other watering places with their cattle and sheep and camels, leaving me three good waterholes for photography. But it was weeks before the game came back. Finally, when I built my blinds I encountered several weeks of murky weather. And after the clouds cleared the country became so dry that every movement filled the air with alkali dust; and then came prairie fires to add smoke to the trouble. I was five months on two safaris before I got pictures. It is about the last word in camera troubles when one has to buy a waterhole to give a zebra a drink—and then gets burned out!

It must be realized, too, that a camera safari is much more pretentious and exacting an undertaking than a mere hunt where one is concerned only with food and ammunition. Photographic equipment alone runs to a considerable weight and must be carried in duplicate to guard against losses and accidents. On one safari, when Daniel Pomeroy was with us, we left Nairobi with six motor cars and about forty porters. We travelled three days to the north and spent ten days trying to get rhino pictures. We saw thirty-nine rhinos in the ten days and got close to many of them—for a moment. But always they got our scent and ran, or they stayed with fiendish persistence in places where photography was impossible, or else the light failed us. We had to leave after that difficult and costly trip without a single decent picture. A few months later we returned to exactly the same region and made a wonderful series of rhino pictures in only three days, photographing them often as close to the camera as fifty feet. There really is such a thing as luck—in Africa.

Long safaris take up a great deal of time in going through gameless regions. Often we have made safaris from Lake Paradise requiring five weeks time to do one week's work. Once we made a long camel safari into the Ndoto mountains when we did not picture one animal. They had all migrated to the Horr valley where we did not dare follow because wild Habash raiders were in there to poach ivory. The Habash do not like to be disturbed at their poaching and there are some chances we will not take—even for a picture.

Perhaps the chief photographic problem in Africa is involved in the keeping of sensitized materials and chemicals. Photo emulsions are made of a highly sensitive gelatine impregnated with delicately balanced silver salt solutions. Conditions of humidity and temperature affect the film which must be continually safeguarded. This means the use of carefully sealed tins, special drying compounds and a continuous supply of fresh stock. I kept a steady flow of shipments coming from the Eastman Kodak plant in Rochester, arriving every few months.

But delivery out in the blue is something more of a problem than it is in civilization.

One thing in particular surprised me on our last expedition: though many months had elapsed since my photographic materials had been packed in America and we had had a bad rainy season, these did not seem to have deteriorated. And all my electric equipment, too, was in good shape. The engines started off smoothly with the first turn of the fly wheel; the electro-light fluid was right on the first testing; and we had lights in the laboratory soon after the building was finished.

My laboratory at Paradise was my chief delight. The walls were high, the entire inside was covered with white canvas, while the canvas on the dark room walls was painted a dark red. Here there were also little red bulbs, developing tanks fed by six inlets of hose running through the logs; and the floor was as smooth as any parquet, for I had had the boys rub the covers of the boxes I used with sand for three days.

My all-important water came from a well dug near the edge of the lake about 30 feet down, and located three hundred yards from my laboratory. Four mules worked from 6:30 A.M. to 3 P.M. bringing the water up. Each mule had a pack saddle that held one "barrimal" on each side. A barrimal was eight gallons. Thus each mule brought up 16 gallons on a trip. The grand total was 800 gallons a day. Any one who recognizes the importance of washing in photographic work will appreciate the value of this investment of good labor.

At the well I had to install a semi-rotary pump in order to bring up good clear water. But, to be on the safe side, every drop was passed through a sand and charcoal filter before going into the barrimal.

When the water reached the laboratory it was poured into a 500-gallon tank which had a filter at its top. There was still another filter at the bottom through which it ran into a 100-gallon tap, and then into the darkroom. I don't think a modern high-voltage generator would have seemed more compli-cated to my black boys than did all this elaborate arrangement of "black magic" I put together for purifying my photographic water.

Of course it was vital to develop all my film right on the spot. I rigged a big tank for the rinsing that followed. A second tank was provided in which the film was cleansed for one hour and a half in running water. Then in a third and last tank the film soaked in water filtered through a special cotton filter I had brought from New York. After fifteen minutes it was then taken to the drying room.

As the film went on the drying drum it was run through some fine chamois skins that had been soaked for days in filtered water. This removed all surplus water and took off the last bit of impurity that might have stuck to the emulsion. But to make doubly sure I then took another chamois skin and ran the film through it again. After this there was small chance of water marks.

When the film had dried and come off the drum I mended it, patched blank leader on its ends and wrapped it in a special chemical proof paper. It was then placed in tins, taped and the entire tin dipped in paraffin wax. This made the package absolutely air tight.

Later, when time was available, I fashioned big canvas caps for our living quarters and for the laboratory. These caps fitted over the entire roofs with canvas gutters which carried rain water to six hundred gallon tanks at the corners of the houses. By this means and with extra tanks I was able to store a reserve of 2,400 gallons.

Of all the things we did I think this home photographic work was least understood by the natives. It is peculiar that even the most intelligent of them cannot understand a picture at first. They turn it upside down and on its side trying to find out what it is all about. I have shown them the best of my flashlights and daytime stills and often they cannot tell an elephant from a rhino.

I had one boy who helped me in the laboratory for over a year. At first the pictures meant nothing

THIS LIONESS RETURNED FOUR TIMES TO BE PHOTOGRAPHED.

Among my pictures I have selected about a dozen that I consider my best. This is certainly one of them. When each picture was made Osa and I would come down from the tree, Osa holding an Eveready flashlight and a rifle, while I recharged the flash apparatus, and each time the lioness would come back within about fifty yards and watch us as we threw the light on her. She probably thought it was thunder and lightning. Of course she was blinded after every flash, but on getting her sight back she would invariably return.

A LEOPARD THAT DESERVED HIS PICTURE.

In the daytime we frightened a lion off the giraffe, and sat up three nights to get a flashlight. But, as the lion never came back, we photographed this leopard on the third night, as this animal had been returning conscientiously every night.

to him. But as time went on the outlines and shadows gradually seemed to make an impression on his brain, and finally he literally became a picture fiend. He could even tell a good negative from a poor one. But it took months for his brain to adjust itself to the flat paper. I think it must have been absence of depth and stereoscopic effect that made the pictures meaningless to him at first.

This same thing holds true all over the world among primitive blacks. A Solomon Island missionary once told me of a new class of raw savages he began to teach. The first lessons were in A-B-C's on big hand charts. As the savages insisted on holding the charts upside down "and every other which way" the missionary got tired of correcting them, hoping it would make no difference later on. However, as time passed the habit became fixed. Finally when the class came to church they sang with their hymn books upside down and read from their upside down bibles. They never learned to read with their bibles right side up!

Toward the end of my stay, when I had my best elephant film finished I sent for Boculy, my elephant guide. I told him to get all the boys up after dark and I would show them what I had been doing for so long. When they came I never enjoyed a film show so much. We gave Boculy a seat on a box next to us and then ran off ten thousand feet of film.

Boculy had never seen a movie before in his life. And up to that moment I don't believe he ever quite understood what our crazy wanderings over the hills and plains had been about. But when he saw all our adventures over again and himself in many of the pictures he was simply stunned by the wonder of it. He kept repeating "*Ah-h-h! Ahh-h-h!*" He was too full of astonishment even to put his emotion into words. He never once took his eyes off the screen and when he saw the elephants close up he was the most excited person I have ever seen in my life. The porters talked and yelled and "*Ah-h-h-d*" for hours after the show.

In closing this chapter let me say that after thirty years of the screen the motion picture is only now coming into real recognition as the paramount medium of record for exploration and nature study. The rapidly improving status of the expeditionary motion picture, in both the lay and scientific mind, and its growing audience, are of special satisfaction to me—especially after having devoted nearly twenty years of an interested but markedly strenuous career to it.

Most of the pioneering has been done. Henceforward we who work in this field have the somewhat easier labor of building upon the foundation so tediously, painfully and expensively laid in the past. The real beginning was with Paul J. Rainey's now classic African Hunt, which was followed by an imitative succession of pictures, good and bad. Then my own South Seas pictures made ten years or more ago gave a certain impetus to the making of films of the far and strange places. Several interesting influences became evident. The motion picture industry became aware, although with some timid reservations, that something beside the synthetic drama of the studios could be considered screen merchandise. Various scientific persons and institutions were made more conscious of the powers and scope of the motion picture camera, not alone as an instrument of interpretation. It was seen that such film was capable of preserving and carrying to its audiences not only the sheer pictorial facts, but also something of the atmosphere and intangible qualities of the subject.

Evidences of this power to infect the audience and the public mind with spirit and atmosphere through the screen are to be found in the very notable wave of South Sea literature which rose following the wide distribution and success of the South Seas pictures.

I am inclined to think that if the contents of the motion picture were the only record, both the public and I would long since have exhausted interest. The larger function of the expeditionary picture is interpretation of the life scenes recorded. Otherwise it would be as empty of color and flavor as a map.

It is also encouraging to note how within the last few years it has become apparent that properly made expeditionary, adventure and nature pictures now have an opportunity, under adequate exploitation, to become largely self supporting. It is true that never since the Rainey pictures has any picture of this type paid such high returns in relation to production cost as the successful dramas of the trade. But I am inclined to the belief that an examination of the records will show that in point of fact, if averages are considered, expeditionary pictures are less speculative than studio products.

It must be borne in mind, too, that the apparent record, with stress on the word *apparent*, is clouded considerably by the fact that a great many expeditionary pictures have been charged with costs of production that ought to have been billed against entertainment and excitement that had nothing to do with the negative. The expeditionary picture has too often been the incidental by-product of a hunt. If pictures are to be made for anything besides the kodak album, picture making must dominate the expedition.

All this is preliminary to stating my enthusiasms for the motion pictorial future of Africa, which now is clearly the "star" continent of screen adventure.

Words have atmosphere and mystic values. "Abyssinia," for example, is one of them; Africa is

AN AFRICAN KILLER TAKES HIS OWN PICTURE.

I shall never forget the morning when I developed this negative. I had set up my flash apparatus for the first time. It went off during the night and I went down and took in the plate. In the morning I watched the spots develop and then, when it came out of the hypo, I ran down the hill to show it to Osa. We thought then—and still think—that it is the best leopard picture ever made. Notice his long tail in the grass.

A DANGEROUS CUSTOMER.

For centuries the African buffalo has been widely regarded as the most dangerous of all big game animals. It sometimes attacks unprovoked, but the real danger lies in following a wounded buffalo into the thick cover it always seeks when wounded. There it often waits beside its tracks and charges without warning. Aside from man, the buffalo's only real enemy is the lion.

another. "Africa" has an exciting, desperate, thrilling connotation. Africa is better material today than ever before. This star value of Africa has been building for many years. It began too long ago to remember. It got its first relatively recent impetus from Paul du Chaillu. Then the tremendously dramatic Livingstone-Stanley story contributed. And there has been a steady increase since, with the journeys of Roosevelt, Rainey, Carl Akeley and countless others. Africa is today better screen material than ever before.

CHAPTER XII

MY WIFE HOLDS THE GUN

THANK heaven I have had the right sort of woman to take along with me into the desert and jungle. If ever a man needed a partner in his chosen vocation it has been I. And if ever a wife were a partner to a man, it is Osa Johnson.

The original travel disease was in me. I ran away when only a youngster and made several trips on cattle boats to Europe. After knocking about there for a while I fell in with Jack London and joined him on his famous cruise to the South Sea Islands in the little *Snark*. By the time I got back to my home I thought I'd satisfied my wanderlust. I settled down in earnest.

I built a playhouse there along the lines of the *Snark*. Those were the days before the moving picture had come into its own. Vaudeville was still more important than the pictures. My chief business rival ran a theatre on the other side of town. I figured his success came from having a wife who could sing. Nothing should do but that I meet this competition by securing a singer.

I heard of a young girl in a nearby town by the name of Osa Leighty who was said to have a good voice. I hopped a train and went up to see her. She was all for the adventure, just as she has been ever since. But her mother was outraged at the idea of my taking away her beautiful young daughter who was still nothing but a child.

That was Friday. For two days Osa and I talked things over pretty seriously. I got a glimpse of her character and I guess she got a taste of my stubbornness. At any rate we solved our problem. On Sunday we were married.

At that time Osa had never been over thirty miles from home. Today I believe she is the most widely travelled woman in the world.

I soon found married life wasn't all a bed of roses. Naturally Osa got a little homesick at first. And her mother missed her a lot. So she had to go home every now and then. These visits often stretched out into days and weeks. Like every other young husband I felt torn between my business and my wife. Also I was dismayed to find that my desire to wander was coming back full force.

One day I put it right up to Osa. "I'm going to sell the business. We can go to the west coast and take a boat to the Islands. If we get some good film it will be worth all the trouble."

It was just about that time Emmet Dalton was

making money in Kansas City showing pictures
duplicating the notorious Dalton raid in which his
father and family were killed.

Again Osa looked hard facts in the face. She knew
that my plan meant choosing between her mother
and myself. She loved both of us and she was a
truly domestic girl. She had never wanted to gad
about or to leave the part of the country in which she
was brought up. She hesitated.

"It will be a tough trip," I told her frankly.

I remember she stood up and looked me in the eye.
A regular writer would say she met the crisis like a
real man. But knowing her, I can say that a real
woman acts just the same way as a real man does.

"I'll go with you, Martin," she told me quietly.
I don't think any man could love a woman more than
I loved her at that moment. I knew how much
courage her decision took.

Don't think we were well off. True we sold out
before we left. But that didn't much more than
stake us to the trip. On the way west I showed
some of my film and gave talks on my projected
voyage to the South Seas. Osa did her share by
dressing up like a native dancer and singing a couple
of Hawaiian songs.

It was on this trip that a new trait showed up in
the girl. Man-like I mixed with other business men
on our way west. I heard a good deal to discourage

me in my plan. I had tempting opportunities to break off and go into other lines of business. Several times I wavered.

One night I explained a particularly attractive offer to Osa in our hotel. "You know we might be barking up the wrong tree," I reminded her. "Maybe it would be better to stop here and look this proposition over."

She hopped off the edge of the bed as if she had sat on a tack. She grabbed the lapel of my coat and gave it a shake.

"Look here, Martin Johnson," she exclaimed. "You are the one who started us on this South Sea Island business. I agreed to go there with you. And that's where I'm going. So don't be flirting around with these other things until we've got this first job done!"

Well, there was no use arguing when she felt like that. Many a time since then she's kept me on a straight course. I think a man's wife can be keel and rudder to him at times.

Osa's tenacious enthusiasm as much as anything else inspired me to do something big. I planned a five reel feature showing life in the South Seas. That wouldn't mean much these days. But at that time no one had attempted anything of the sort longer than one reel. I chose the title "Cannibals of the South Seas." Osa confessed afterward that the very word "cannibal" made her shudder. But she never winced at the time.

Nor did she wince when, a little later, she was captured by the savage man-eaters we were out to film.

We sailed west in a small ship. I knew Osa was brave. But it took more than bravery to combat seasickness. To my joy she didn't have a single hour of illness. To this day she has never known what that scourge of the sea-traveller is like, despite the tiny craft and terrible storms we have gone through in our wanderings.

"Oh, yes, she's got a strong stomach," said an older woman scornfully once when I mentioned it.

But I don't believe this is the whole truth. I think Osa's profound delight in our work and the thrill with which she looks forward to our next adventure adds enormously to her bodily resistance to ills that overwhelm the diffident tourist. To my mind she is an excellent sample of mental state governing health.

We got into trouble with the cannibals through my own rashness. Our destination at the time was the island of Malekula in the New Hebrides. Government officials warned me against the natives. "They are our subjects on the map," explained one officer. "But a cannibal doesn't know a map from a kangaroo."

About all the effect this advise had on me was to swell the mental picture I had of my film's future earnings.

I won't go into details. It isn't a pleasant story. But Osa and I landed on Malekula full of confidence. It was all jungle surrounded by a coral beach. We foolishly went right in among the black savages and began to film them. We got separated and were taken prisoners. Osa was led to a village and I was headed for the pot. Luckily the commanding officer of a British man-of-war, on hearing of our projected visit to the island, got worried and came after us. He effected our rescue just in time.

Naturally I felt a little conscience-stricken for having gotten Osa in such a mess. "Had enough of this?" I asked her soon afterward.

"Have you got the film you came after?" she retorted.

I confessed I hadn't.

"Then let's get it," said she firmly.

How could a man fail with a wife like that?

Now that we were both broken in and knew our cocoanuts, so to speak, we chartered a little yawl and went up among the Solomon Islands. On the *Snark* Jack London had shown me the most interesting spots of this charming group.

Osa had her troubles from the outset. I had hired a black boy to cook for us and the crew. The second

day out he developed an infected hand. As a result
our single lady passenger had to work throughout
the voyage in a two-by-four galley preparing meals
for us both. Frankly, that was one job I couldn't
have begun to have done.

In all we cruised over six hundred miles clear up to
the southernmost of the Solomons, Owa-raha Island.
Osa helped me with the photographic work when she
had finished with her pots and pans. We both slept
on the teak deck. Our camp equipment was so
limited that while ashore we bunked in native huts.
Had it not been for Osa's courageous example I am
not sure I could have stood the dirty grass houses and
odoriferous natives.

"I've smelt worse right in civilization," she laughingly told me.

Her biggest thrill seemed to come when we crossed
afoot the Island of Malaita. In a way the trip was a
sort of stunt. No white people had ever been across
before. Also it promised to give us priceless views
for the film we were slowly building. We should
never have been able to go except that a government
exploring party was making the trip and the leader
was kind enough to invite us along.

I remember he called me aside and inquired anxiously: "Are you sure your wife can stand it?"

"Pretty sure," said I, smiling to myself.

"How do you know?"

"Well, if she can't, I certainly can't!" was the best reason I could think of.

It was a rough trip all right. Every moment of it we were in danger from the wild tribes that haunted the jungle through which we plodded. Our army of black boys were just as frightened as we were; more so, in fact, for they knew what it meant to be tortured by the cannibals.

Here it was that Osa first began to develop her natural talent for rifle shooting. I call it a talent because she had never done any shooting as a girl. Yet with a few days practice she began to bring in pigeons, wild goat and fish as a result of her marksmanship.

Another trait she brought forward unexpectedly was her quick mastery of native lore. In no time she picked up a smattering of local dialects and spent long hours over our campfires listening to tales of hunting and superstition. As the years have gone on she has developed this hobby until she speaks Malay and Swahili fluently and has endeared herself to natives of many tribes by her sympathetic interest in their lives and beliefs.

Just about the time we began to feel at home among the Solomon Islands we had an experience that nearly ended our adventuring forever. The little vessel on which we were cruising had to go back to get more supplies and to pick up the British commissioner.

Osa agreed to stay with me ashore while I went ahead with my work.   I should say she *insisted* on staying, because I don't believe she would ever desert me even if I tried to force her to go.

We had just landed on one of the smaller islands. We didn't know it at the time, but several white people had been killed there by the natives shortly before.

As we disembarked in the dark the natives didn't know we were there.   Next morning they were holding some kind of fiesta.   With fine innocence we decided it was a good chance for pictures and boldly entered the crowd.   The first thing we knew a perfect bedlam broke loose.   Women screamed and about two thousand wild and wholly naked men came dashing up to us armed with spears and poison arrows which they brandished in the air while they screeched at the top of their lungs.   We had our guns ready.   Osa did not flinch.   But it would have done no good to fire, we were so outnumbered.

Later we learned that it was the confusion which saved our lives.   There was so much racket that when a wild rumor spread among the natives to the effect that there were more of us around the point, they believed it and fled.   Providentially our boat returned at this critical moment and took us off.

When we had recovered somewhat from this close call I tried to make light of the experience by saying

THE MODERN SHORT SKIRT IN NEW SURROUNDINGS.

These young ladies of fashion are all members of the Chuka tribe which resides along the slopes of Mt. Kenya.

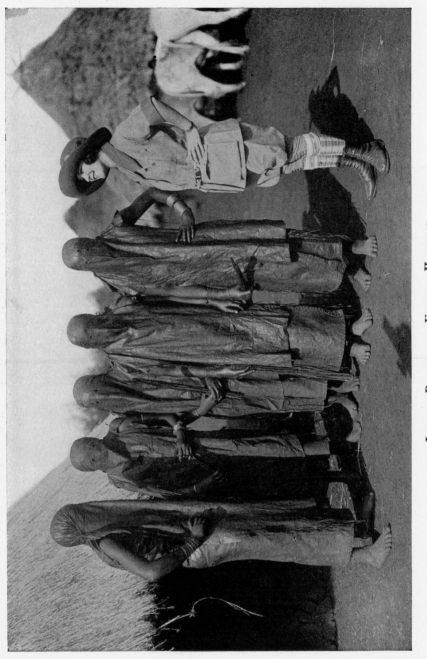

LUMBWA DEBUTANTES UNDER A HANDICAP.

Girls of the Lumbwa tribe must don this queer Ku Klux Klan dress for six months. After that, they are circumcised and married. This group formed a consignment destined to be married to one old chief.

to Osa: "Well, how did you like those fellows?"

She shook her head and smiled one of her knowing smiles. "They're not nice people, Martin," she said, "And you know they're not." That was her only comment.

I thought the poor girl was going to have a rest after that harrowing experience. But we made a foolish mistake a few weeks later that got us into almost as bad a jam. We visited the Leuneuwa Lagoon about three hundred miles further north where the tribes are not so hostile to white men. But they are very superstitious. When Osa followed me into one of their "devil houses" there was literally the devil to pay.

No woman was ever allowed in one under pain of death. The natives couldn't understand us and we didn't know a word of their tongue. So for days it looked as if our lives weren't worth five cents. Finally things quieted down and we were able to get away with whole skins. Why, we never knew.

During these years I learned that a healthy woman has just as much vitality as a man. I always had good health and plenty of muscle. But often when I have been ready to give up in despair Osa has been still full of pep and ready to go on.

I remember once when we got caught out in a small open boat among the islands. The weather was tough and we had practically no food. The black boys with us were ready to beach the boat and take a chance on being marooned. I am frank to say that I had about reached the same state of mind. But not Osa. She picked up her gun and held it on our mutinous crew. "I'll shoot the first boy that goes over the side," she told them. And the tone of her voice showed she meant it.

Do you wonder I hate to see the way women in America are so often pampered and spoiled when I know how fine they are underneath their surface polish.

Many a doctor has told me that a normal woman's endurance is the equal of any man her age. I have seen Osa come in scores of times after a hard day in the field when I could hardly drag one foot after the other, and go to work in the kitchen seeing that the evening meal is being cooked right.

After a visit to Australia and the Malay Peninsula, with some exciting times in Borneo, we finally drifted down into Africa. There I chose a permanent field for my future work, which is preservation of wild life in film form. Africa is the last large unspoiled country where one can find game as it was before mankind spread around the globe, ruthlessly driving all life before him.

By this time Osa was thoroughly imbued with a love for the outdoors. She was a better shot than I, got along splendidly with natives and loved travelling through the wilderness with a passion equalled only by my own intense pleasure in animal photography.

By happy fortune we discovered a lovely and long lost lake up in the Kenya country in the crater of an extinct volcano. Four years ago we made our second long visit to Africa and built a permanent home on this water which we named Lake Paradise. There, surrounded by wild elephants and black half-naked savages Osa entered her latest adventure in outlandish domesticity.

For many weeks after our arrival I watched her curiously. Before we had always come home. Now we might *visit* back in the States, but our true home was in that far corner of wildest Africa.

As usual, Osa ran true to form. She entered into the spirit of the whole project from the very start. When we erected our main lodge with logs hewn from the forest and a roof thatched from native grass she built her boudoir with her own hands.

This boudoir was a nice big cool room fourteen by sixteen feet, or nearly as large as an expensive hotel room in New York. She laid the floor herself from some fruit boxes we had among our stores. While I was busy getting up the laboratory she directed the plastering of the walls with mud—native fashion. This doesn't sound very nice when you read it. But if you could have seen how firmly and hard that African clay dried, and how attractive it was when

tinted a light rose pink by a wash made from a light
dust one of the native maids found in a near-by
bank, you would scarcely believe that the whole
interior had not been planned by some famous
decorator.

Inner partitions were made of slender sticks cut
green and woven into artistic designs. Little items
like towel racks Osa made herself out of odds and
ends left over by the native builders. She painted
her bathroom white with many coats until it gave
a soft milky glow when the sunlight filtered in
through the shade trees without. She even built her
own tables and one or two of her lighter chairs. She
had never looked on herself as carpenter before.
She started the jobs at first just to kill time while the
men were tied up with their building operations.
But she soon found that it was one of the most
fascinating games at which she had ever played.

She planted a garden with sweet potatoes and
asparagus in it. She tended the chickens and ran the
dairy where we made butter from fresh milk provided
by the cows we bought from the natives.

She shot quail and guinea hen on the trail. She
organized our laundry force. She taught the blacks
to cook meat and bake bread. She was my commissary steward; not an easy job five hundred miles
from the nearest grocery store.

In the serious work she also took a very serious

part. She handled the gun while I cranked the camera.

Twice she has dropped elephants at my feet.

Once a lion came charging for me in the open with swift powerful springs. I dared crank because Osa held the gun. At fifteen feet she fired. The enraged beast stumbled but came on. She fired again. This time she dropped him so close I could touch his mane with my toe.

The feeling that Osa is so accurate a shot means a lot in my camera work. I am usually intent on the focussing and speed of film, and often do not even realize the danger facing us. Osa stands there coolly, gun in hand. If the game is too quiet she wanders forward cautiously and stirs it up. She seems to have no nerves.

Let me quote a typical passage from Osa's diary. She went down to the lake one morning and met one of those little adventures which would likely be upsetting to a woman not used to the jungle, but which to Osa has become just routine.

"On my way back," she says, "I climbed down through some dense growth to the water's edge. Just as I emerged I heard a thud and the breaking of a branch a few yards away. I glanced up and found myself looking into the beady eye of a huge elephant. He was just as surprised as I was.

" 'Don't move,' whispered the black with me.

"Believe me, I couldn't move. I was rooted to the spot. The funny part was that Martin on the other side of the Lake happened to pick up his binoculars and see me through them at this very minute. There was nothing he could do. Anyway he knew me well enough to realize that if the elephant came for me I'd go up a tree like a cat. Many a time I was treed by rhino or elephants within earshot of our house.

"The elephant didn't seem a bit angry or worried. He waggled his ears and switched his little tail about and just stared. I think he'd have scratched his head if he could have, he looked so puzzled. Finally, he decided to see what I would do if he went away. So he backed into the forest a few yards until he was out of sight. That was my cue to go. I quickly slipped away along the shore. A few minutes later I looked back. The elephant had returned and was drinking quietly without looking up."

Another time she wrote:

"Much of our diet came from the forest. I used to wander through the heavily timbered land back of us and pick up wild asparagus, wild apricots, mushrooms and so forth.

"But I had to keep my eyes open. One exciting morning I had just located a nice patch of mushrooms when I heard a crash and a snort behind me. I whirled about expecting an elephant. There stood

one of the largest rhinos I think I have ever looked at.
He was furious.   He pawed the ground and swung his
head to and fro.   I knew he was going to charge.

"A rhino doesn't wait around and think things
over the way an elephant does.   His temper is too
short.   Almost before I could jump for a tree this
fellow started for me.   Luckily I found a low branch
before he reached me.   I climbed as high as I could
and sat quietly but quaking.   After a lot of pawing
around and snorting the old scoundrel finally decided
he was outwitted and left.

"I never did get along with rhinos the whole time
we were out there," she goes on to say.   "Somehow I
was always getting mixed up with one.   And they are
such irritable ill-mannered beasts that I dislike them
as much as they seem to dislike me.

"One day I had been out with Martin after elephant
films.   We had had an unusually good day.   We
were returning to our camp outside the forest which
held our village.   We had just come out into the open
from some brush when an elephant turned up.

"'You go on, Osa,' said Martin.   'I'll see if I can't
get a picture or two."

"As the animal was off the trail it looked as if I
could pass him unnoticed.

"I took another trail to be on the safe side.   Martin
circled around and in about fifteen minutes came
over toward me.   He roused a rhino on the way.   I

was riding a mule. The first thing I knew the rhino and mule saw each other at the same time. And both were scared.

"Then began the strangest race in history. The trail was narrow. And both beasts had to follow it for a while. I hung on for dear life while the rhino tried to escape the mule and the terrified mule tried to escape the rhino. As the rhino was a little behind it would have been the end of me to have fallen off. Finally the rhino beat the mule and I was saved."

Nevertheless, I had to leave Osa with an exacted promise not to stray far from camp without Ndundu, the gun-bearer, and a threat to Bukhari, the headman, to skin him alive if he didn't guard her. The threat, however, was almost unnecessary, so far as our boys were concerned. All were devoted to her; and Bukhari would sooner have lost his own life than hers. The Nubians, the most aristocratic of African races, are all that way. Up in their north country, a Nubian guide simply cannot return to his village if he comes back with a single soul missing from a party he has taken out. It is a matter of honor and tradition with the race.

Even if it were not, Bukhari's character is such that he would die for her. And he is a splendid-looking fellow, with his strong reliable features, his fine head and muscles that ripple over his arms like little rapids of the river over boulders. None could

A FINE TYPE OF MERU.

Songa, Chief and son of a chief, represented the finest type of Meru nobility, which
was borne out in both his features and bearing.

A NECKLACE MADE OF ELEPHANTS' TAILS.

We estimated that the tails of at least twenty elephants went into the making of this Samburu lady's necklace. The Samburu people belong to about the lowest tribe in East Africa—a homeless tribe which migrates with the grass and water over the face of the Kaisoot desert.

be more considerate than he in little things and the same held true of many of the boys. If Osa came in tired, they had the pot boiling on the camp fire and soon had a cup of tea ready. And they continually watched out for wild animals and let her take no unnecessary risks if they could prevent it.

I have never seen the porters' eyes so vigilant on the grass and path for those coiling cobras as when she is along. Sometimes when I have berated them I think they would have liked to see one strike me; but there would be such a wail of native mourning go up from the camp that all Africa would hear if anything happened to Osa.

There is no question about it, ours was an unnerving life for a woman. As all the rest of us were men I suppose we didn't half give Osa credit for the shocks her femininity must sometimes have received. For even though she was the best sport in the world about it all, she was still a woman.

I remember one day we were jolting along in our trucks over the awful trail near Mt. Kenya on the way up to Lake Paradise when the car Osa was driving jolted over something soft and yielding.

"Martin, Abdullah, come here. I've run over someone!" she screamed.

Coming to a stop with a jerk, I ran up, and flashed my pocket lamp on the body of a native boy who appeared to be about fifteen years old. His face was slashed and so was his throat; insects were crawling in the coagulated blood; and when I turned him over we saw that his back had been slashed very deep.

Osa was trembling.

"It is not your fault," I said to comfort her. "We can charge that to leopards."

But I had jumped to too swift a conclusion, for Abdullah shook his head and said in gruff Swahili: "Nothing that walks on four feet, something that walks on two, did for him, Bwana."

I next examined the *kapandi* in the little case around his neck. This is the official document, or working paper, which every native must carry to show who is his present employer, who his last, and is a great aid in catching deserters. I was glad to find that it was not one of my own boys. Still, that was small relief, for it opened up the possibility that one of my force might have been the murderer. And to back this murder theory we found, clutched in his hand, little pebbles with which the boys sometimes play a crude game of chance.

I remember one ugly experience we had with elephants when only Osa's nerve saved my life. She was terribly frightened, just as often a brave man is frightened. But in spite of her fear she stood by her guns and made it possible for me to be alive and write this story today.

This happened before we built our Lake Paradise

home.   In the early days on a former expedition, I used to collect a little ivory occasionally.   One day we came on a small herd in an open space that promised easy shooting.   Looming above the females was an old bull with a fine long gleaming pair of tusks below his chin.

None of the elephants saw us.   I whispered to Osa to stay by the camera while I went in closer for a shot. I knew there was a good chance of some interesting film if one of the beasts charged me.

As I crept forward I kept my gun at ready.   One can never tell whether an elephant will charge or run away and I did not want to lose my tusker.

Suddenly the big fellow glanced up and saw me. As I was very close, I fired.   I thought I had hit him in a vital spot.   Indeed, had Osa been the hunter, the victim would probably have fallen then and there. But somehow I missed the small brain area which the bullet must penetrate to be fatal.

The bull jumped and charged.   I ran at top speed toward Osa.   She was cranking the camera, getting priceless film as I fled for my life.   It may seem to the reader that she was callous in letting the charging elephant come after me and doing nothing about it except take my picture.   But her quick eye caught the fact instantly that the elephant was not gaining much.

The great danger to me lay in the possibility that I

might stumble. Osa knew this as well as I. More
than once she had had to run over rough ground to
escape rhinos. Also holding my rifle and glancing
over my shoulder made my movements awkward.

Out of the corner of her eye Osa kept watch on her
gun-bearer. This was a black boy whose duty it was
to remain at her elbow and hand out her rifle in
emergency. Here again she took a chance because
the natural impulse of the native was to flee.

Of course the other elephants in the herd came
after the big bull. That is the instinct of most
animals which travel in groups. The sight of the
huge lumbering beasts pounding along in a charge
that was meant to wipe us all off the map was enough
to make anyone shiver. I think Osa did more shiver-
ing than I because she was standing still and could
see more.

She cranked as long as she dared. Then she
reached down and grabbed her gun. Under ordinary
circumstances I like to see her shoot. She has a
natural grace about her whole act of marksmanship
that is rare. But this time I was in no mood to
appreciate anything but escape.

In a split second she had the rifle to her shoulder
and fired. I swerved as the mortally wounded
elephant thundered past and fell with a thud that
shook us all.

Seeing that the others of the herd were checked

and that our danger was over I stepped up to Osa for a word of admiration.   She was very pale.

"I—I guess I have to sit down for a minute, Martin," she said.

I didn't blame her.   My own knees felt a little weak.

To Osa I attribute in a large measure the comfort and efficiency of our camps on safari.   She it was who as commissary officer of my party worked out much of the routine as well as the food supplies.

Near noon we usually stopped and rested men and animals in whatever shade might be available. Then we would be off again soon after the sun had crossed the meridian.   The order to stop in the evening came enough before sunset to give plenty of time to make a proper camp.   While we were un-packing, our personal boys made a quick fire and hot water for tea.   As soon as this was ready we sat and sipped it while the other unpacking went on apace. We didn't sit on the ground and hold our cups in our hands.   We sat on folding chairs and our cups were placed on a folding table.

By the time we had finished our tea, our baths were ready in our individual tents.   Osa never left out her bath at this time of the day, no matter how tired or discouraged she was.   To step out of a tub and into fresh clean garments that had been laun-dered and ironed and laid out for one was like starting life all over again.

Now the sun was nestling on the horizon. Long purple shadows were creeping over the plains. The night cries of wild animals had not yet begun. On our little table had been laid a snowy white table-cloth. Napkins and spotless porcelain were at each place. *Hors d'œuvres* were served as we took our seats. Then came a simple soup and an *entrée* with vegetables. If we had been away from the base less than a week we had a salad of fresh greens out of my garden. A sweet of some sort usually topped off the meal. Thus we ate a balanced diet, and we ate it in the most tranquil and contented state of mind.

We have never had to fight to keep down weight. I weighed 207 pounds when I left America. In nine months I was down to 164, all good hard muscle. Osa dropped from 130 to 115 pounds in the same period. She wasn't thin either; and she said she never felt so well in her life as she did when she had gotten rid of that excess fat.

Before Osa went to bed in her roomy cot with its clean sheets, she rubbed her face thoroughly with a good dose of cold cream. With the help of her native maid she always did her hair completely before break-fast out on the trail as well as at home. In the early days of our stay she selected this girl herself. The negress was a six-foot girl of the Boran tribe which lived a good ways beyond our district. She was twenty-four years old, black as tar, with broad shoulders and a fine robust figure. Her name was the rather unpronounceable one of "Guyuaka." Properly used it sounded not unlike the quack of a duck.

This girl's duties were to take care of Osa just as a maid would at home. Of course she didn't know the first thing about a white woman's life. But she was willing and interested, and she took a childish pride in everything Osa did. As time passed she became more and more devoted, until she was worried every time Osa went out where lions or elephants or other dangerous big game might be met.

One night Osa had gone further from the base than she had meant to go. I was away on another party. It was very dark and Osa was alone except for her gun-bearer and several native hunters. Now and then big shadowy animals crossed the trail ahead of them. When a rhino came too close, the boys scared him away by shouting at the top of their lungs. Every minute Osa expected a leopard to spring at them through the high grass.

When the party reached camp, Guyuaka was waiting up for Osa with tea. Her hand shook as she held out the cup and it was plain that she had been crying. When Osa questioned her she found out that the black had heard gunshots out on the plains and was positive that Osa had been attacked by wild beasts. That night Osa awakened and found the maid kneeling by her bed praying to the Boran

Gods to protect her mistress from the terrible things for which Osa had no proper respect or fear.

In everything Osa did she tried to be as normal as possible. She wore no fancy hunting costumes, yet always had a change of color, even though slight. Nice browns and grays were her favorites.

I think she tried to see life through the eyes of the wild animals we photographed. When they resented our presence in their domain, Osa, like me, grew to understand how they felt and to be tolerant of their anger. Neither of us had to try to like the natural joys of our life, good plain food, plenty of exercise and as much laughter in our waking hours as the law would permit.

All these things boiled down into a sort of philosophy of contentment. To this contentment, rather than to any single item of my régime, we attributed our perfect health.

You wouldn't think Osa could keep her feminine looks and personality in such a life as we lead. But she does. Her photographs show how young and fresh her expression is. (An acquaintance who doesn't know her has suggested they might have been taken before she went to Africa. But these were taken on her last trip.)

I think her perfect health has more to do with her looks than any other single factor. Next comes her enthusiasm for our work. Her habits are regular and she always has plenty of hard work on hand. When she is in the field she often rides and walks fifteen or twenty miles a day. At home she is continually tinkering with her garden or about our house. She rises early and goes to bed soon after dark.

She is not introspective. Indeed, I have never known a person to think so little of self.

I have been asked if it is much of an effort to keep Osa from the pursuits of other women. I confess that she is normal enough to like pretty clothes and bridge and dancing. Sometimes at home in America I have a sneaking fear that such things are weaning her away from me and our work. But there always comes a time when she secretly slips back to me and whispers: "Oh, Martin, I'll be so glad when we get back to Africa!"

People wonder what Osa and I talk about on our long safaris often with no companions other than the hundred or so black porters who handle our camels and carry our baggage.

We talk much about the things that mean the least to us. In human beings there is always the desire to know what the other fellow thinks. We talk about America and wonder what the folks are doing back there. We talk of happenings of the day. So-and-so did this or that wrong; we must tell him not to do it again.

We do less talking together than people in civilization. We are so close and our companionship is so perfect that I think we exchange many thoughts without words.

It means a lot to have a real partner in one's life work.

CHAPTER XIII

VISITORS AND ILLNESS

WHEN Fate gets good and busy we poor mortals must take her lashings as best we may. Our last eighteen months in Africa, which should have been our best, were in some ways our hardest through no fault of our own. I think the toughest time Osa and I went through together was during the only serious illness we have ever had. And while the siege came after the events I shall presently relate, I am going to describe it first because it illuminates the difficulties the tourist may face if he strays too far from the beaten path. I think we escaped death only because we were too well seasoned by many years in the field.

For years snow-capped Mt. Kenya had been beckoning us with a white finger across the wide plains. Finally in our fourth winter of our last expedition we set out to climb to the top of the mountain and make films of the snow and ice up there in contrast to the elephants and other tropical animal life we had so faithfully recorded.

We sent seven mules, fifteen porters and three

syces ahead to a base camp near the foot of the mountain in early January. On the 14th I sent fifteen more. And the following day we set out with our faithful Willys-Knight trucks and Osa's new "Six" for our climb.

On the 16th we reached Chogoria Mission, on the slopes of the mountain. There we talked over our plans with Dr. Irwine and his wife who were staying at the station. On the same afternoon we continued on up the ascent for about five miles more. Near our camp we found two Swiss aviators who were flying from Switzerland to the Cape. Their machine had broken down near Jinga on the Lake and they took time for a climb while repairs were being made.

On the 17th we signed on about fifty Meru porters with the help of Dr. Irwine. Our assistant, John Wilshusen, went into Meru for blankets, as we had to give every one two. We had to get "Gee" in petrol tins to take the place of meat. To supply my Nairobi boys and the Meru porters I had to buy nearly a hundred and ninety blankets.

Early in the morning of the 18th we set out. We climbed continually up through most beautiful forests with rhino, elephant and buffalo spoor everywhere, but we did not see any animals. The boys had to rest every thirty minutes for the grade was very steep. At 5 o'clock we camped at the edge of a bamboo forest in a most beautiful clearing which

was one mass of color with wild flowers.   Before dark
it was so cold that the boys huddled about their
fires and we wore our overcoats.

On the morning of the 19th we entered the bamboo.
There was not another tree of any kind; nothing
but bamboo about fifty feet tall and so dense that
daylight scarcely filtered through.   Five boys went
ahead all the time to clear the trail.   *Bonga* tracks
were all over the place but I don't see how anyone
could hunt them, for it would be almost impossible to
get through the forest without cutting; and dry bamboo on the ground cracked like firecrackers.

About noon we suddenly came out of the bamboo
into scrub country.   The bamboo forest was most
interesting in as much as it started suddenly and
ended suddenly, with no straggling at the edges.
From noon to about four o'clock we went through
the most beautiful country I have ever seen anywhere; rolling plains with beautiful groves of scrub
trees which were loaded down with moss.   Kenya
loomed ahead with rugged beauty.   By this time
the wind was very cold, although the sun shone
brightly.   We had the most peculiar feeling; hot
and still cold.   I mean by this that without sweaters
we were chilled, but by bundling up with sweaters
we would sweat; and if we took off our hats our
heads would get hot.

At four we left the timber line and came into short

grass country with boulders and stones all over the place; no trees, but lots of small scrub bushes with gnarled roots above the ground. Thirty minutes after leaving timber line we came to what was called the first rest at 12,000 feet.

Before going further I will describe the origin of these rest houses. A few years ago, a Mr. Carr, who is a retired millionaire jam manufacturer from England, with three hundred porters, spent several months in clearing a road through the forest. His idea was to make the road direct to the snow line. But this first rest house was as far as he got. Here he and his porters erected a portable house that looked like the portable garages we have at home. As they could not get the road further they carried the other rest house up a few thousand feet and erected it, but winds have blown it away.

We did not use the rest house that night; but had a tent set up. It was so cold that we could not sleep. In the night the boys started coughing and muttering for they, too, were sleepless. In the morning our basin was frozen over, and both Osa and I had bad colds. Five boys had fevers of over 103 and I had one of 102. We decided to rest a day and start on the next, as I was in no condition to walk. Here we left the mules, as the grade was almost straight up. It got our wind so badly that we could only walk a short distance at a time. Besides, we had to rearrange the boys' loads, as they could no longer carry a full sixty pounds.

After lunch I felt better. Osa and I with porters carrying cameras started up the trail to see what we could photograph. I think it was this trip that did us in. For in trying to reach a ridge where we expected to get good pictures we over-exerted ourselves and climbed all of two thousand feet. As we were further away from camp than we thought, we did not get back until after dark. We were chilled through by then and both went to bed without dinner.

In the middle of the night our temperatures went up again until I had 104 and Osa 102. We called the boys and had hot water bottles prepared and hot whiskey made. But by morning we were very ill with fits of coughing. Osa's temperature kept rising and her breathing was so fast that I was badly frightened; so much so that I offered heavy *baksheesh* to a couple of boys to hurry down the mountain after Dr. Irwine. I suspected that Osa had pneumonia; and I knew that I had bronchitis.

Two boys and John Wilshusen went but found the doctor away. However, John was equal to the emergency. He gathered all the porters he could scrape together—twelve I believe—armed them with pangas, and started up the mountain with the Willys-Knight big six. This trip of his will always to me be one of the biggest things I have ever known. With the boys cutting, digging and pushing John reached us on the second night, with the top nearly off the car, boxes ripped off by the trees, front mudguard badly dented and one canopy stanchion torn off, but with the car in good running order. John had had almost nothing to eat and was covered with grease and dirt. His porters were all in.

During this time Osa and I were the most miserable couple on earth. At nights Osa was out of her head and I thought she would die any time. John kept hot water bottles going and hot whiskey. The only medicine I had was aspirin, which was not what I needed.

John arrived about nine o'clock at night. In the morning he and the boys made up a bed for Osa and me in the back of the car. We set off down the mountain on a wild trip. Before that we sent off boys in relays so we could pick them up at bad places to push. We also had ten boys riding on the sides of the car. We left posho and many other things behind.

The descent was awfully bumpy. We had to get out of the car about eight times at bad places. This was the worst to us. If the reader has ever seen anyone with pneumonia he will know what it was like to have to take poor Osa out of the car at a time like this. But we had to do it because there were

AT A STATION ON THE KENYA AND UGANDA RAILWAY.

Myself, Osa, George Eastman, Daniel Pomeroy, and Dr. Audeley Stewart.

SNOW-CAPPED MT. KENYA AS SEEN FROM NANYUKI.

There is always snow on Kenya, and sometimes the entire peak is covered. At other seasons, only a small amount is seen. Running from Kenya are small clear cool streams that have been stocked with both brown and rainbow trout. They afford the finest trout fishing in the world, and are the only places on earth where the fisherman can glance up and see elephants or rhino or buffalo watching him.

places where we expected the car would turn over.

We reached the Mission at dark. Dr. Irwine had been sent for and a grass house was fixed up with beds. Osa seemed a little better when we got into the house; but my fever was a hundred and four. The doctor said I had bronchitis on top of influenza. Osa had double pneumonia and in a short while was delirious. Dr. Irwine was frightened and sent John off to Meru a little after midnight, where he sent wires to Nairobi for another doctor. On getting word that Dr. Anderson had set out, John returned. Dr. Irwine then said a nurse was necessary at once. So John set out again for Nairobi and did the hundred and sixty miles in five hours and twenty minutes. He was lucky in getting a nurse and returned in another five hours. The nurse says her hair turned gray on this trip.

On arrival Dr. Anderson found another nurse was necessary and more medicine. John arrived with the first nurse and immediately turned around and rushed back to Nairobi for another. As he could not find a nurse in town he made a sixty mile trip out into the country and got her and was back with us early next morning.

I was moved out of the hut into the Mission while both doctors and a nurse and the doctor's wife worked over Osa all night. Before daylight Dr. Anderson came in and told me he was afraid Osa would not live. He asked for her mother's address so she could be wired as he thought he should prepare her. A runner was sent to Meru with the wire.

I got out of bed without any one knowing it and slipped into the grass house, where the doctor and Dr. Irwine were applying ice cold towels to Osa's body. It was the most heart-breaking sight I ever saw. Osa was unconscious. Her eyes were wide open, her lips a ghastly blue and her breath was so fast that it was horrible. She would start coughing and gasp for breath. After each coughing spell she seemed to be dying.

In the morning she slept a little and seemed much better. But that night the doctors were again afraid and told me to be prepared. She might die any minute. And the next night it was the same way. They would not allow me out of bed for I was very ill myself. But many times each night I slipped into the grass house before they could stop me, though Osa never knew me.

When John arrived with the second nurse the doctors mentioned what a God-send ice would be. Whereupon good old John rushed again into Nairobi and got an ice machine and rushed back with it. Then he made ice as fast as he and the boys could. He had fixed up the machine so that it worked perfectly, and was able to make ice in less than three minutes.

John and the wonderful Willys-Knight absolutely

saved Osa's life and perhaps mine too.   For a week I
never knew of John's sleeping or eating.   He never
had time to wash up.   The crisis came a few days
later when Osa suddenly took a turn for the better
and in the most remarkable way started to improve.
By February 15th I was on the road to recovery
though still weak as a cat.   And I knew at last what
it meant to be ill in the field.

As I have said, I go into some detail in describing
the complications of our illness because the traveller
must be prepared for emergency.   This especially
applies to those who are not accustomed to a country.
And it is for this very reason that I felt a definite
responsibility whenever any of my friends came out
from America to visit us.

News of our most prominent visitors reached us by
runner at Lake Paradise.   He brought a telegram
telling us that Mr. George Eastman, Mr. Daniel
Pomeroy and Dr. Audeley Stewart were arriving
in Nairobi intending to pay us a visit.   We also got
word that Carl Akeley and his wife with their group
of painters and taxidermists had arrived in Nairobi.

We hastily packed our "chop" (food) box and set
out to meet our friends.   About one hundred miles
from the Lake we camped at a water hole on the
Kaisoot Desert and left our motor cars to be picked
up after we had made a week's safari over the Ndoto
Mountains.   We hoped to find elephants there, but

were disappointed. While we were away we ran out
of water and had to resort to a small mud puddle
that was being used as a rhino and buffalo wallow.
We drove the beasts away and had the boys bring
enough of the mud into camp for distilling with the
little still we always carried for the purpose.

After a disappointing jaunt we returned to our
motors and worked on down to the Guaso Nyiro
River. Finding it in flood we camped on the banks
for three days. Then there appeared on the opposite
bank a Boer convoy rider. He had ten wagons and
nearly two hundred Abyssinian donkeys. He was on
his way to one of the distant military posts with
supplies. We knew we must go on or miss the
Eastman party. So we made a deal with the Boer
to send us across a long cable hitched to thirty-five
donkeys. This cable we made fast to the motor cars
and had them pulled across. The stream was so swift
that all the machines were drifted downstream
and badly buffeted on the other bank. One had two
wheels broken off at its axle and the steering gear
ruined. But after twenty-four hours of hard work
I found myself and Osa on the far side with all our
belongings. It took several days more to put our
cars back into running order again.

The mud was so bad that on the first day we made
only four miles and then became hopelessly bogged.
I sent back for the Boer and made another deal with

him whereby he was to stay with us until we were out of the worst going. After that for a week he towed our cars through the mud at intervals. One we had to abandon hopelessly bogged.

Osa and I went on, sloshing through the mud for two hundred miles more to Nairobi, completing the worst safari I think we ever experienced. At Nairobi we had a reunion with Carl Akeley who had rented a big stone house on the outskirts of the town and was preparing for the arrival of the Eastman expedition. The latter came in on the following day and for the next week we were busy getting their things out of customs and preparing for our first safari with them.

It was now raining every day. We had planned to take the newcomers directly back to Lake Paradise; but we knew it would be hopeless to attempt the trip at this time. This reminds me that I have heard the seasons in South Africa are changing somewhat. Certain it is that the rainy and dry seasons in Africa seem to have gotten mixed up. They don't start any more where they should; and neither do they end on schedule. However, such conclusions should not be drawn hastily from only a few seasons' observations.

As the Kedong Valley, about thirty-five miles out of Nairobi, seemed to be dry, we took our friends down there for ten days. This valley is part of the great Rift Valley, which starts in Asia and zigzags down through the entire continent of Africa from north to south.

It was in the Kedong Valley just a few days before our visit that there was a terrible encounter with rhinos reported. I can do no better in describing the tragedy than quote from the Nairobi paper of May 4, 1926, which read in part as follows:

WHITE WOMAN CHARGED BY TWO RHINOS

Mrs. Bailey, wife of Mr. G. L. Bailey, of "Sterndale," Naivasha, is an inmate of Nairobi European Hospital after being the victim of an experience which comes within the lives of few women. She owes the fact that she is still alive to some miraculous intervention or accident of which she is quite unaware.

While hunting in Suswa, the mountain which rises above the great Rift Valley and is one of the breasts of the Queen of Sheba in the mythology and ancient history of Africa, she was charged by two rhinoceroses and very seriously injured.

This is the thrilling story of her adventure.

Mr. and Mrs. Bailey were on safari and had established their camp near Suswa for a week. On the night before the accident they had been sitting up for lions, and Mrs. Bailey caught a chill. On the following day she decided that she would not go far and she intended to spend an uneventful day hunting around the camp for reedbuck with a small rifle. Mr. Bailey departed with a gun-bearer to seek

game on the plains and Mrs. Bailey, with another
bearer and a second native, decided to climb Suswa.
She found no sign of reedbuck and set out to return to
camp.

On the way home she discovered fresh tracks of
rhino and suddenly came upon two of the animals
lying down under a tree in more or less open ground.
She hurried to camp and brought her husband's
double .470 rifle and the natives back to the spot.
When she arrived she found that the two animals
had changed their position and were resting under a
thick bush.

Mrs. Bailey crept slowly forward until she was
well within forty yards. The rhinos were in such a
position that one was practically covering the outline of its companion, and she supposed they were an
old rhino and a full-grown youngster. The latter
was nearest to her and she fired at the rhino on the
farther side, choosing as a mark an exposed shoulder
to get a heart shot.

The next thing she knew was that they both rose to
their feet and rushed through the bush at her,
charging side by side. Mrs. Bailey's one and only
thought was that the end of her life had arrived, and
she had no time to turn about or fire a second time.

One of the animals caught her with its horn on her
side; the horn travelled right up her body and tore
away the whole of the scalp on that side. She was
thrown high into the air among the trees, and when
she came down the rhino trod upon her as she lay on
the ground.

Both native gun-bearers stood the strain well.

They were experienced men, and they kept their ground. As soon as opportunity offered they lifted the injured woman up—her face streaming blood—and when she regained her feet, she discovered that one of the rhinos was rapidly returning. The natives dragged Mrs. Bailey into a dry water gully, and the gun-bearer drove the animal off with rifle fire. Then they set out to carry Mrs. Bailey four miles to camp and luckily met another party of the camp porters who had been in the same locality for the camp water supply. Among them they brought her down, quite unconscious, and one native hurried on ahead to inform Mr. Bailey who met the party bringing his injured wife about a mile from camp.

On this trip Mr. Eastman used a shower bath of his own devising that deserves mention. It is rare that the explorer and traveller, no matter how he bathes, can have a real shower in the field.

The device consisted of a regular collapsible automobile canvas pail to the bottom of which was attached a hose fitting. From the fitting led a four-foot length of soft rubber tube, near the end of which was a clothespin to regulate the flow of water. Every evening after the day's hunt Mr. Eastman's tentboy, Abdulla, hung this pail on the front tent pole about head high, put the zinc bathtub underneath and filled the bucket with warm water. The rest of the operation was left to the owner of the mechanism.

PHILIP PERCIVAL AND GEORGE EASTMAN TALK IT OVER.

Philip Percival, with pipe, and George Eastman, at Camp at Karo waterhole on the Kaisoot desert. Percival is one of the outstanding big-game hunters of Africa and a most delightful safari companion. Mr. Eastman gets every bit of enjoyment out of safari life, and takes the keenest interest in camp activities.

Mr. Daniel Pomeroy with His Impalla.

Mr. Pomeroy, with Mr. George Eastman, spent several months with us. This is one of the finest impalla I have ever seen. It has by far the most graceful head of the smaller antelopes. Mr. Pomeroy secured some of the best specimens for the American Museum of Natural History groups, to be placed in the new Akeley African Hall. He did very little shooting, but the specimens he did shoot were perfect.

To give an idea of the organization of a field party of the sort we were now working with I list the following:

	Natives
Philip Percival, white hunter, boy and gun-bearer	2
Osa and Martin Johnson, two boys	2
Pomeroy, boy, gun-bearer and skinner	3
Stewart, boy, gun-bearer	2
G. Eastman, boy, two gun-bearers and skinner	4
Chauffeur and helper (Boer)	1
Head man (this is the man who had one eye clawed out by a leopard in the Stewart Edward White party)	1
Cook	1
Porters	12
Syces	2
Total Natives	30

Total Whites—7 (including chauffeur who is a Dutchman and eats by himself).

Mr. Eastman is, of course, one of the industrial leaders of the world. Imagine our surprise when we discovered that he had not devoted all his talents to the perfection of the kodak. We found him an expert cook who could prepare for us on the camp stove coffee, biscuit, muffins, graham gems, corn bread, lemon tarts and huckleberry pie as good as we had ever eaten. Percival offered the millionaire six hundred dollars a month and all the hunting in British East Africa if Mr. Eastman would henceforth direct the cuisine of his safaris.

"I'll accept if Mrs. Johnson will join up with me," laughed the latter. But I demurred at this point, declaring that I could not afford to lose Osa, my own commissary officer. So the scheme fell through.

On May 29th we left the Eastman party to go on to Lake Paradise and prepare for its arrival. We had been away for six weeks and wanted to be sure things were in order for our guests. We had a special house built for the occupancy of Mr. Eastman; and had the blacks put their own part of our little "village" in apple-pie order.

As usual, there were some adventures for the new-comers which Osa and I did not have to stage. On June 6th we visited a place called Karo where the only water had to be dug out of the dry bed of a river. There I had a blind from which I hoped to give Mr. Eastman a look at some animals as we often saw them, undisturbed by any knowledge of the proximity of man. But we had no luck.

The next day I thought I'd try another spot. On the way there we came up with an old rhino grazing alone quite unconscious that we were in the neighbor-hood. Mr. Eastman nervily got within twenty yards of the beast, taking pictures as he went. But a

moment later this approach proved a little too daring.
The rhino suddenly looked up and charged without
the usual preliminaries.   Luckily Philip Percival and
I were ready with our guns.   At ten yards Phil let
drive.   The rhino fell about six yards from
Mr. Eastman.

The same night a lion got into our mules at camp.
This was a little more nerve-racking than it sounds.
For the mules were tethered right in the middle of
the camp between our tents and the boys.   The lion
somehow got his claw into the jaw of one of them
and nearly did for it then and there.

Luckily the boys waked up with a chorus of howls,
at which the surprised lion beat a hasty retreat.
The wretched mule broke away in its agony but
turned up next day still alive; how it escaped being
eaten during the night I cannot say.   Its jaws were
terribly swollen and lacerated.   But it got well
eventually.   The next night a leopard got into camp
but did no damage.

By this time our visitors began really to feel they
were in "Darkest Africa."

After about two weeks we all got underway for the
south again.   Near Lesamis Osa and Mr. Eastman
devoted some time to one of their favorite sports,
that of shooting sand grouse for our camp table.   At
the waterhole here the birds could be got both night
and morning, hundreds of them coming down to

drink at sunrise and sunset, as regular as clockwork.

A pause was made here for a camel safari of 28 camels. These could carry food and equipment for ten days for the big party which we now made, and water for four days. Since we now had 61 natives and 7 whites this was doing very well. Water was the troublesome item. That at Lesamis was dirty; and we had only 14 gallons left from the supply we took on at the Lake.

When the time came to pack and go, the camels, who are never on their good behavior—if they have any—acted a little worse than usual. Four or five kicked off their loads and disturbed the whole caravan. It was nearly four in the afternoon before we finally got underway.

Game proved fairly scarce on the journey. Also the weather got hotter and hotter, the temperature going up to well above 90°F. in the middle of the day. Elephant were seen but no decent pictures secured, much to the disappointment of the newcomers. On July 3 we gave up the search for game and struck out for our base camp at Merille where our cars were waiting to take us down to Nairobi. Thence the Eastman-Pomeroy party made a trip down to the southwest after lions, some of the adventures of which we shared and which I will presently describe. It was these adventures which made the high point of our four years.

Another bit of visiting came with Sister Withall, the trained nurse that accompanied us while Osa was convalescing after her pneumonia. She and Osa struck up a great friendship. We finally asked her to go out on a short safari with us. She had nursed all over the world, Australia, New Zealand and South America. She was among the first six nurses to go out from England to Belgium when the war broke out; and she was one of the last to leave when the Armistice was signed. She married in Mombasa after demobilization, her husband dying six months later.

At the time the doctor said he thought it was unwise for us to take a hard trip on account of our condition. He approved of my suggestion that we try a safari out on the Kaisoot Desert for a time. John Wilshusen, who had saved our lives in the Willys-Knights, was available and willing to go with us. So he brought the cars down to Chogoria Mission station and helped make a bed in one so Osa could travel.

We promptly headed toward the desert and were soon out of sight of the little station that had sheltered us through our miserable siege. Not three miles away we ran into a pig hole. While we were getting the car out Osa discovered two rhino slowly walking towards us. At once I left the car with my camera and unlimbered for some pictures. It was not until the animals were within forty feet of us that they discovered our presence. For a moment

I thought we were in for a charge. The rhinos pawed the earth, snorted, looked undecided, then turned and ran.

When I looked around there was Sister Withall and Osa. They had moved the car slowly up, stopped and climbed atop it to watch the fun. This was Osa's first outing from being bedridden since she had been taken ill on the mountain.

A few days later we reached a waterhole that had proved promising in the past. In the afternoon we set up the cameras and were about to begin a wait for game when down the trail trotted a big bull rhino that came to within fifty feet before he saw us. He stopped, gave a snort and galloped our way with his head down. Fifteen feet from the camera he whirled and ran around a tree. Osa, still a little wobbly, but ready with her gun, watched him closely. Sister Withall was palpably worried.

After circling the tree the rhino apparently decided we were just an hallucination and decided to come on down again. This time he dashed along at full speed and showed every sign of charging right through us all. To save our lives Osa fired at twelve feet and brought him down with this single round from her .405 Winchester.

After the incident Osa returned to camp and went to bed. The excitement had been too much for her convalescent state.

The following morning we built a blind for flash-lights. Lions were roaring all about us all night and it looked as if we might get something good, though we were supposed to be on vacation. Again in the afternoon we all wandered out to the waterhole to see if it were being used. Hanged if we didn't have the same experience as we had had the day before. Just as we got set a rhino came charging down upon us and didn't stop for men, women, camera or anything else until Osa was forced to fire at a distance of about fifteen feet, bringing the lunatic down at the very last moment. This time she went back to bed again for two days. Sister Withall exclaimed: "One more rhino charge and she'll be on her back for good."

I forgot to mention that Osa now had a new maid. This one's name was the usual unpronounceable kind. She had been brought to our place under peculiar circumstances. Quite some time before, a Boran had presented himself at my laboratory door with my gun-bearer, saying that he had a cow and calf for sale; that he was on his way down country and the calf had just been born. He wanted to sell the cow and the calf to me. I learned that the price was seventy shillings; as this figure was a fair one I made the purchase.

When the transaction was over, one of my porters stepped up and suggested that, as he had saved quite a sum of money, he would like to buy the Boran's daughter. I had long ago learned that one has to be careful with the native women coming into camp. We never allowed more than two or three around at a time. If we got the wrong kind we always had trouble, for with so many boys around one wild black lady could almost break up our organization. The girl was now brought in. And as she didn't look like a trouble-maker I gave my man permission to buy her. I even furnished him the sixty shillings to pay the bill, as I owed him more than that.

The interesting thing was that the Boran should sell his cow for seventy shillings and his daughter for only sixty. The porter was very good to the girl; and a short while later we took her away from his menage and attached her to Osa as personal maid. In the end she became a devoted and efficient servant.

After Osa got thoroughly on her feet again she became restless. She came to me one morning and asked if she might break the set rule of Lake Paradise namely, that not one shot should be fired in the Lake district. She wanted to get a Greater Kudu, the true aristocrat of the African forest and one of the most wary game animals on the list.

At first I thought I should refuse. I couldn't get away to go with her and knew that she must face the dangers of the forest alone except for her helpers.

WARRIOR AND LION SPEARED ON THE SERENGETI PLAINS.

Usually the lion finds enough zebra and other food to satisfy his needs. But at the end of each rainy season, when the plains game migrates, he is a menace to the natives' stock. Lion cubs are spotted; but I never could detect these markings with my eye. They always, however, showed plainly in the finished picture; and while they often seemed to disappear as the cub matured, photographs sometimes reveal them even on the old lions.

AFTER A LION SPEARING.

Osa with one of the Lumbwa warriors who had distinguished himself at one of the most savage sports we had ever seen.

But finally I gave in and her chop boxes were packed within an hour.

In the following days she wandered all over the highest peaks in the Lake Paradise region. The Kudu is found mostly near the tops of mountains. From what the boys said afterward Osa led them on a safari that even I would not have tackled. On the second day she sighted a beautiful specimen. For six days and nights thereafter she tenaciously followed it without ever getting within rifle shot. On the afternoon of the sixth day she managed to get within three hundred yards of the Kudu. She dropped to her knees, took careful aim and brought him down dead at the first shot. At this moment a giant cobra rose up directly in front of her and nearly scared her to death.

She was half the night getting back to her camp, running into two herds of elephants on the way. I was in my laboratory when she came in the following day. She entered with a woebegone expression that told me she had failed. I began to sympathize, being only too glad that she had come back safely. I followed her into the next room and there, to my astonishment, saw propped up on logs one of the finest of the rare kudu heads I had ever set eyes on.

Two days later natives came in to tell us of a wounded buffalo, probably an animal that had been speared and got away. The natives said this same buffalo had killed an old woman and a young Boran boy, and had badly wounded another native that had been out herding sheep. I did not have time to go out after the animal. I knew it ought to be killed, for there is probably no more dangerous animal than the buffalo in such a state. Nor did I want Osa to go after it.

But the Boran said that the beast could be found in the crater of an old extinct volcano, where we could sit atop a rock and shoot it as it walked out. Osa had never been after buffalo. And when she heard that there might be some excitement she was all for going. Finally she dispelled my apprehensions and set off with the same boys she had taken on her Kudu hunt.

She spent three days in the chase. She saw the buffalo every day at the bottom of the old extinct crater over on the edge of the Kaisoot Desert where it seemed to live. But she couldn't get at it on account of the heavy brush thereabouts.

Finally on the fourth day she got a bunch of Borans camped nearby to take their half-wild dogs and form a drive through the bush in order to drive the buffalo towards her. The drive was successful in short order. The buffalo came charging down upon the rock where Osa was perched. She jumped off and ran directly in the path of the furious animal. At ten feet she let him have a bullet from her 405.

Probably she has never made a more dangerous shot in her whole African life. Had the bullet not hit just right it would have ricochetted and done no harm. Further, had the animal not been so close I doubt if the bullet would have penetrated, for the point she hit was tougher than bone itself.

When we finally returned from Lake Paradise with the Eastman-Pomeroy party to Nairobi we found waiting for us John Wilshusen and three new Willys-Knight cars, one a big six and two one-ton trucks. These cars were what we considered the very best for the fearfully rough usage we had to put them to.

On the day they were ready we all prepared for our trip down to Tanganyika for lions, the Eastman party going on ahead of us. We were filled with anticipation at the prospect of this safari, but little did we realize what tremendous things were in store for us in the next few weeks.

Best of all, I think, Carl Akeley was to be along and share with us his wonderful store of African knowledge.

CHAPTER XIV

TANGANYIKA LIONS

"THE lion is a sportsman and a gentleman. He attends to his own business and will leave you alone so long as you leave him alone. Man slaughters him in cold blood because the lion was created and ordained to live on flesh. Yet man kills nearly every animal to eat."

So did Carl Akeley speak to me one dark African night on safari not long before he died and was buried in the hills and jungle that he loved so well.

The lion is a cat. You must never forget that. But if you are a person who has never seen a live lion in his own haunts, a lion unaggravated by the ruthlessness of man, you will know him only through the catch-phrase, the twisted legend and the humiliating still-picture of him as he lies helpless in death. You will think of the lion as a cruel, treacherous, bloodthirsty beast of prey. You will imagine him slinking through the underbrush toward his victim. You will picture him crunching flesh or roaring, a ruthless enemy of all other animal life.

It was now in our third year when we went south

JUST BEFORE OUR MOST EXCITING ADVENTURE.

Osa, myself, and one of our cars among the Lumbwa natives. Lions had wrought havoc among the cattle of these people the night before, and we arrived just as they were dancing and getting ready to go out and spear the marauders. We interrupted the ceremonies a few minutes and then they went back to their ngoma. Next day we accompanied them on their lion spearing expedition—the most exciting adventure we ever had.

SURROUNDED BY LUMBWA WARRIORS.

These people were on the lion trail at the time, and paid very little attention to us. In fact they resented our presence in the country while they were at work. They could not understand cameras and we often got in their way.

to Tanganyika that we had what we now term our "Great Lion Adventure." Probably in our hearts we, too, thought of lions as cruel prowlers of the jungle. Nightly we heard them roar about our camps between the waterholes. Time after time we came on gruesome evidence of their handiwork in dead half-eaten giraffes and zebras. Fleeting glimpse of their tawny bodies in grassy dongas often made us grip our rifles tighter.

Several times we had a taste of the lion's ferocity when disturbed.

One time, Osa, my wife, and I were out on the sun-baked veldt travelling with our native gun-bearers and with porters carrying our motion picture cameras. We were not particularly looking for lions, although we knew we were in lion country.

We had passed countless tracks of game, criss-crossing over our route; but there was a curious absence of actual animal life which was significant.

I suddenly began to pick up bits of low conversation from the natives with us. They were speaking of the dreaded simba (which is the native word for lion). Just then, as if fate chose to endorse their apprehensions, there appeared right ahead of us on the rough floor of the desert the brownish shape of a huge crouching lion.

The lion's tail was switching about like a flag in the hands of a railway guard—his warning signal.

This left no doubt in our minds about his mood. He was angry at our intrusion. He may have been stalking his prey; he may have been asleep; he may have been courting when we chanced by. It made no difference. He was thoroughly enraged that our party had blundered upon his activities and dared still to come his way.

I knew enough about lions not to go on. Quickly I had the big camera set up and Osa got hers out of its case. The gun-bearers took their stations a little behind and on both sides of us to be ready in case of trouble.

Scarcely had I started to crank when the beast began his advance. His tail was flipping violently from side to side; now and then he gave vent to a harsh growl of anger.

He didn't charge all at once. He would advance a few yards, then lie down in a tense crouching position. He seemed to be working himself up into an uncontrollable rage. Six times he repeated this performance while I recorded his movements by film.

Finally he could no longer control his desire to annihilate us. He was just a hundred yards away and right out in plain sight in broad daylight when he rose and charged.

I can't say I enjoyed standing there turning my crank during that rush. It was the most beautiful, and at the same time the most terrifying sight I think I have ever seen. He looked almost as big as a full grown bull as he came tearing down upon us, his mane flying and his dripping teeth bared for the final death-dealing assault. The black boys were ready to collapse when Osa fired. The huge body checked for a split-second in mid-air, then fell and rolled to a point just thirteen feet from my camera's tripod.

Once more there was impressed upon my mind how surely was the lion but a gigantic murdering cat, far better dead than alive.

It is only fair to add, however, that even at this time I was not afraid of being eaten by a lion. The belief that a lion is a man-eater is generally incorrect. Lions enjoy zebra and giraffe meat best of all; human flesh does not usually appeal to them. In my six years' residence in Africa in lion country I have never been able personally to trace an authentic case of a man-eating lion. Often I have heard of them; but, when I run the facts to earth they always turn out to be nothing more than wild rumor.

It was Phil Percival who persuaded us to go far south into Tanganyika Territory for our best lion adventures. This section of Africa is on the lower eastern border, well south of Nairobi. It is well protected by natural obstacles, since it is a rough and nearly waterless country. Its isolation is, I think, the chief reason that it is probably one of the most wonderful game tracts in the world.

Not long after we entered it we fell in with forty naked Lumbwa warriors in war paint also out after lions. With them we had another chance to see the big cats "at their worst." The native hunters were armed with long spears and small elliptical shields covered only with buffalo hide. Each man had his own idea of war paint both on himself and on his shield.

When we came up the blacks were in a state of great excitement. For days they had been working themselves into a fever of courage and exhilaration in order to nerve themselves for facing simba in his own haunts. I must say I admired their boldness in deliberately planning to fight lions with weapons as fragile as theirs and with no sort of defense against the animals' poisonous claws save their hide shields.

The purpose of the hunt was not for trophies or for meat. The native does not eat lion flesh; nor has he any use for the skin save that he uses its claws in his amulets. The whole movement was a defensive one; a sortie against lions that had been attacking and carrying off the black man's precious cattle.

We paused to watch some of the killings. We saw six in all. It was a thrilling nerve-racking performance.

First the natives ranged out in a line of advance scouts. When a lion was located in the grass or brush the scouts retreated until joined by their brothers. A sort of rough semicircular formation was then taken and the advance began.

Meanwhile the lion usually behaved somewhat as the big fellow did who charged Osa and me. He lashed himself into a fury at the intrusion of man and prepared to fight any who dared approach him. Only twice did I actually see one run away; and that was when he was pressed hard from all sides and many times outnumbered. Even then he did not give the impression of running away. He simply changed his course and disappeared at a powerful trot which gave the impression that he had important business elsewhere.

Occasionally the lion would make off as if he had decided that his duties were not as important as those of the strange two-legged beasts who had suddenly cropped up on all sides. But when he discovered that it was himself whom they pursued he did not hesitate to turn and engage the enemy with spirit.

At the first sign of the lion's determination to charge, the warriors paused. This was the dramatic high point of the scene; the crouched lion with lashing tail ready to charge on the slightest provocation; the tense and naked black men with glistening spears raised in the sunshine and trembling in their almost unbearable suspense.

Then a superb plunging rush by the King of Beasts. The black line held. What magnificent courage it takes to stand unarmed, save for a slender little spear before a charging lion, only one who has stood with chilling blood and watched it can ever realize.

With a last mad roar the lion sprang. Simultaneously a salvo of spears shot from a score of hands. Taking the tearing claws on their shields the nearest blacks crouched low. Others rose full height and added their shafts to those already buried deep in the flesh of the quivering torso.

A brief dusty mêlée, the dying lion and sweating blacks miraculously intermingled; then the long drawn cry of triumph from the warriors.

More than once I saw the lion maul the spearsmen in these fracases. More than once it was clear to me that the lion was fighting with his back to the wall, at bay, knowing the odds were against him; yet he fought on, and died fighting.

It was with these impressions behind me that I entered Tanganyika, combining my party with Carl Akeley's. We camped on the edge of the great plain that sloped gently upward to the mountains. We knew we were going to get lions. Nightly they roared about us. But as yet we had encountered none of the herds that we had come so far to see.

Next day Phil Percival came in with a wide grin on his face that meant success. Quickly he told us what he had found on his reconnoissance. "Not lions," he said first, for he knew how eager we were. "But plenty of other kinds of animals." He had struck the vanguard of a big game migration at a point not many miles away. Luckily the movement seemed to be in our direction.

Next morning we broke camp early. Our own excitement communicated itself to the natives. Rarely had they packed so quickly before. We worked our way down through the most beautiful country I have ever seen: wide stretches of plains, broken here and there by grotesque rock formations that suggested a lunar landscape. The chief vege-tation consisted of little forests of thick thorn growth. Otherwise there was cover neither for us nor for any other animal.

Then we struck game. It was a sight that made us hold our breath. Miles and miles of the wilde-beest in herds that must have numbered into the tens of thousands; Thompson's gazelle more numerous than I had ever seen them before; hundreds of Grant's gazelle; giraffe—sixty-one in a single herd; wart hogs, topi and kongoni; ostriches; innumerable zebras, with an outer fringe of hyenas and jackals numbering hundreds. There were many vultures too, circling high overhead on tireless wings.

It was a hunter's paradise. Game birds were plentiful. The boys caught catfish running as high as fifteen pounds, from pools along the river-bed we skirted.

But still no lions; I mean lions such as Carl Akeley and I had been hoping for; lions that could be studied and photographed while they were unmolested. Carl had for months been promising me I would change my mind about the big cats if only I could once see them his way. But I confess my previous encounters had made me more and more skeptical.

A few days after our arrival in the game district Carl came into camp late in the evening. He had been away all day on a scouting party of his own. I could see he was laboring under some excitement. Almost immediately he took me aside.

"I've found them!" he exclaimed.

Instantly I knew what he meant. Lions!

"Now you'll believe what I say!"

Never had I heard him speak more earnestly. Indeed I was for starting at once although I knew it was absolutely out of the question to dare travel in the darkness away from the protection of our camp fire.

I could scarcely sleep that night. Years before in New York, Carl Akeley had sat in my apartment playing with Kalowatt and talking lions. In his studio in the American Museum I had sat and watched him modelling them. Wherever we were or whatever we discussed he sooner or later prayed that I might some day see with my own eyes what lions really were.

We turned out next morning with the stars still lit; velvet night except where a little of the dawn slipped up over the eastern horizon. We carried guns; but at Carl's behest we agreed not to shoot unless absolutely necessary.

"I don't believe this herd has ever been disturbed," he again declared. But still I doubted.

For hours we moved across the dry and rocky plain. A blazing tropical sun rolled over the edge of the world and struck us heavily with its rays. Dust sifted up from underfoot and bit like acid into our panting nostrils. We were drenched with sweat.

In mid-morning we followed Carl up a slight rise and entered a shallow depression between two hills. Suddenly he paused.

"Here it is," he said and pointed ahead.

At that very instant I saw a brownish shadow disappear into the grass that fronted a small donga or ravine on our right.

We proceeded. Soon we saw another lion. He seemed to be passing on a course opposite to ours. He did not even look our way. Did he fail to see us? Or was Carl's wonderful promise coming true?

Then abruptly and without the slightest warning we came upon eleven full-grown lions. I gasped. All of us stopped in our tracks. We had never dreamed of any sight like this.

Some of the lions were squatting on their haunches; some were crouching; others sitting or lying. Two were taking the air from the top of a five foot ant hill. One was lazily yawning under a big mimosa tree. All looked our way as we came up; but none showed any more concern than might a Sunday crowd in a Central Park exhibit if two or three more loafers drifted up to enjoy the sunshine.

I suppose Carl's heart was beating like mine as we moved slowly forward. We stopped every few feet and made photographs. For we were still not sure how long the beasts would tolerate our presence.

We were about a hundred yards from the lions when we first sighted them. All were out in a little clearing with only some short grass in sparse patches between us and them. When I set up my Akeley camera and started to grind out film the slight noise of the mechanism caused the animals to prick up their ears. But a moment later all looked away as if to prove we meant nothing in their lives.

Up to this point we had spoken only in whispers. In my excitement I forgot and spoke aloud. Instantly every lion faced us. Several rose to their feet with their tails lashing. But after a few low growls of annoyance they quieted down and again began looking in every direction but ours.

Presently they commenced to go to sleep. It was a hot sultry day and their hunting the night before must have made them drowsy. The four directly in front of us lay on their sides. After they had completely lost consciousness they began to roll over with their yellow bellies uppermost, breathing heavily. The one nearest us snored in a low rhythmical undertone.

I had to pinch myself to believe that these were the same species I had seen only as fighting snarling maniacs, crouched with lashing tail or ready on the instant to make a murderous charge.

As the minutes sped by and the lions took less and less notice of us, my heart gradually ceased pounding like a trip hammer. Every now and then Carl would look up at me and bare his teeth in an "I told you so" grin.

We moved forward a few feet at a time. As we continued to shorten the distance between us and the lions, a few of them who were still awake raised their heads, or rather turned them from side to side, because their heads were upside down due to the animals being flat on their backs. But their glances were lazy, blinking looks containing not an atom of hostility. Finally every lion was asleep—eleven full-grown beauties.

We were wondering what to do next when out of the nearest donga came another lion that apparently did not feel as sleepy as his friends. He stood there for a few moments glancing at them slyly. Then he walked up to a big male that was sound asleep and snapped at one of the paws waving in the air. With a roar of surprise and anger the owner of the paw sprang to his feet ready for anything. But when he saw he had been tricked he yawned widely and rambled grumbling away to lie down again and complete his nap.

The joker walked on among the other ten lions, waking up one after another until the little glade rang with growls and snarls of irritation. He paid no attention to us even when he got among the four right in front of where we stood. Finally he lay down beside a sleeping lioness and began to torment her. The poor lady wanted to sleep but he kept right on mauling and mouthing her until she simply had to sit up and maul back. After a few minutes of this both quieted down and began affectionately licking one another.

About this time the biggest lion of the bunch, who had been sleeping with his legs in the air, got slowly to his feet and stretched, yawning a yawn so large that we all wanted to yawn too. He walked over to another spot and flopped himself on the ground so hard that he gave a loud grunt as if he had knocked the wind out of himself.

Not wishing to take advantage of the magnanimous indifference of the lions we backed off and found a big mimosa tree some distance away where, sheltered from the heat of the high blazing sun, we sat and lunched. For four long happy hours we lay about and talked lions. I had never seen Carl Akeley so elated. He was overjoyed to think he had at least proved to me lions will not molest a man if not molested first. Little did I think it was the last long talk I should ever have with this great man.

"This valley has probably never been shot over," he said. "Notice how sleek and well-fed these fellows are. Probably they hunt in packs and have no trouble in getting all the food they want." He paused for a moment of reflection. Then he added: "They have never been whipped; no wonder they're afraid of nothing on earth."

I was out next morning at daybreak with fresh film and porters ready to visit our Lion Valley again. But Mrs. Akeley reported that her husband had a high fever and could not go. On entering his tent I could see he was a very sick man. He seemed to have a presentiment he would never get well. He didn't.

He said: "Go ahead, Martin, and play the game with the lions and they will play the game with you. Get all the data and the pictures you can; then tell the world about it. I want the world to know how unfair it is for sportsmen to slaughter large numbers of lions simply to get a big pot."

Carl's illness gave Osa her chance to go with me. She had been nearly frantic with curiosity after hearing our story of the lions who didn't mind men. She dressed quickly and we set off at top speed along the trail to our Garden of Eden.

At first we came on only single animals and pairs. But about nine o'clock we suddenly found fourteen scattered about near the spot where we had seen the group the day before. I turned and watched Osa's face. It was worth coming all the way down to Tanganyika to see it light up. She held her breath at first; and her voice shook with emotion when she exclaimed: "I never dreamed I should see anything so beautiful in this world!"

Cameras were made ready as before, and porters sent back so we should not seem too big a body to the animals. Slowly we moved toward the lions who watched us curiously.

This time they were more restless and alert; perhaps because the day was cooler. As a result the situation was so dangerous that it needed but a few bounds from the nearest of the powerful cats to finish us off. Of course we had two guns; but as I was busy with the cameras, Osa held the only rifle that was ready.

After we got so close we could not make decent pictures by reducing the distance we began to use different cameras and lens combinations to be sure

we had recorded all the times of this unprecedented
scene.

The lions kept moving around too. Once two
stood on their hind legs and wrapped their fore feet
around one another as they pretended to fight. They
roared and swayed with a most terrifying reality as
they went through the mock combat. One walked to
a tree where, standing on his hind feet, he sharpened
his claws on the trunk. One picked up a small stone
in its fore paws, and tossing it into the air, played
with it as a kitten will play with a ball of yarn.
Several were busy taking their morning baths by
licking their fur exactly as a cat would do. One
seemed to have a thorn or chigger in his toe. He
spent half an hour trying to get it out. I thought of
the fable of the man who took the thorn from the
lion's paw and of the way he was repaid by the lion.
But I did not have the nerve to try it.

After an hour of this sort of thing, Osa suddenly
nudged me and motioned violently behind us. I
turned to find that three more lions had come up
along our line of retreat and were standing but a few
feet away quietly watching the photographing of their
friends. They lay down as we looked at them and
several of the others began to skit around to where
they were.

In three minutes we were completely surrounded
by lions.

About eleven o'clock the animals began drifting down to a nearby donga for their noonday siesta out of the sun. Soon we were left alone, safe and unharmed.

We returned to the shade of the big mimosa tree where our porters were waiting. The natives treated us almost as if we were gods. They had seen us surrounded by lions and could not understand for the life of them why we were not attacked.

After lunch and a short nap Osa went out and shot a zebra. We hoped we could get the lions to focus more in one spot and give us even better pictures than we had taken, so the boys dragged the zebra to a point close to where we had last seen the lions. Then we sent them back out of the way while Osa and I moved up close to the carcass with the cameras.

About five in the evening an old grandmother lioness came out and sniffed at the dead zebra. But apparently she was not hungry, for after inspecting it well with her nose she lay down beside it and went fast asleep. I never knew lions were such sleepy animals.

Now a young lion came up and the lioness left. He rubbed against the zebra and purred; then he lay down beside it until the lioness returned. This time she decided she wanted to be left alone. She lashed her tail and growled, telling the young fellow, who was probably her son, to get away, which he

THE ETERNAL TRIANGLE IN A WILDERNESS SETTING.

This picture shows two males and one female. They are fully grown, but the males have not yet developed big manes. It is doubtful if they ever will, as they are constantly getting the hairs full of thorns and burrs, which they comb out with their claws, pulling out the hairs at the same time. It is seldom that a wild lion has a mane as good as those in zoos.

A Detail of my Strange Experience with Akeley.

There were eleven lions asleep here as Carl Akeley and I came up to them. At first they got to their feet and lashed their tails, then, when we did not move closer, they lay down again and inside of an hour they were all asleep. They paid no attention to the noise of the cameras, but whenever we spoke to one another they were all instantly awake.

promptly did. But she in turn was soon ousted by a big lion which I took to be her husband.

It was getting late and we were ready to go home when another big lioness came along. She soon showed she was in no mood for social amenities. She sighted us at a distance of about a hundred yards and at once came bounding toward us. We retreated quickly to show her we didn't want to interfere. The minute we moved she stopped and lashed her tail angrily. Then she came on again. Once more we retired and she followed.

Of course we could have shot her. We had our rifles all ready in case she made it necessary for us to resort to them. But we did not wish to shoot and spoil the wonderful adventure of Lion Valley.

Finally she seemed to realize that we were determined to get out of the way if she would only give us the chance. I think the trouble was simply that she had seen us hanging about her diggings all day and was tired of our presence. Four times we stopped and four times she came at us, then lay with lashing tail and watched us while we ran. Meanwhile in the distance we could see other lions who had left the chasing entirely to the lioness. I will say she made a good job of it, as we didn't have the nerve to go back.

We paid a number of other visits to the place; and we studied lions at close range to our heart's content, filming them until bankruptcy threatened my celluloid supply. Never was there a tragedy; and not a lion were we compelled to kill.

So it was that I became a convert to Carl Akeley's creed: "The lion is a sportsman and a gentleman; he attends to his own business, and will leave you alone as long as you will leave him alone."

CHAPTER XV

THE END OF THE TRAIL

OUR four years were drawing to a close. On our last Christmas at the Lake Osa lighted her little Christmas tree and the candles seemed to shoot their beams out over the desert from the roof of the world. For the boys we had a barbecue of roast ox, and doled out khaki cloth and cigarettes after dinner.

For ourselves Osa and Phishie prepared a great feast. We had sardines for *hors d'œuvres*, a soup from tomatoes in the garden, "Tommy" (Thompson's gazelle) steaks, roast spurfowl, string beans, alligator pears, apricots, black cranberry sauce, olives, raisin biscuit—Osa's specialty—sweet potatoes, native coffee, floating island pudding, of which we never grew tired, pecans and Nairobi cigars.

After dinner we watched the boys dance and chant, while the flames lighted up the lake and the vine-clad cliffs, their orange red lances piercing the aisles of the forest far beyond the boma. We felt a little happier, I think, for not having neglected Christmas.

Other people had by now found the way to this

sequestered lake, which we had been the first to discover after the missionary who came here two
hundred years ago. And several were still to come.
Some came by the wilder route, like Pat Ayre, the
famous hunter; others, like our good friends Colonel
and Mrs. Bray, who had voyaged from America
all the way to see Africa and us, by the new trail
Boculy had found and which was easier for camels
or cars.

It was pleasant to have the Brays. The Colonel
was a delightful reconteur, and his negro stories, tales
of old Kentucky and of the Keith circuit, of which he
for a long time had been manager, sounded queerly in
the wilds but were a delightful change after so many
yarns in Swahili.

Osa, too, had fixed up her living quarters and guest
house admirably. In the guest room were towel racks
and all the little knicknacks which a woman will
put up, if you give her twenty-four hours in a place;
and they served the purpose, even though they were
made of materials gathered out of the forest. And
woe betide the luckless houseboys if they did not
have sheets and towels, as well as our garments,
freshly laundered every day or two.

The living room was now as comfortable as that
of any country home. There were guns and horns
on the wall; skins on the floor; lounging chairs, most
of which I had made; bright rugs; and always a fire in

the cool of the evening. A fire, too, without soot or much smoke, because the only wood in the forest was hard and gave out a most comforting warmth and color—yellow, often turning to driftwood blue. Seated there in the evenings, it almost seemed as if that civilization which we had tried to escape had caught up with us again.

I think the Brays had a good time during the two weeks they were with us. Certainly they had a glimpse of kaleidoscopic African life. They got mixed up in a rhino charge; a large herd of elephants raided our garden while they were guests; and it was during their visit that the incident I have already related occurred, when one of our boys had a fit, jumped into a big campfire, and was burned so badly that he had lockjaw and died. Unfortunately Mr. Bray fell into a hole early in his visit and sprained his ankle so badly that he had to be sent to Nairobi for medical attendance. On the day of his return my head man came to me and informed me that one of my boys, a Boran herder, seemingly in perfect health had walked off into the forest in the middle of the afternoon when he should have been at work. He was found the next morning dead, with no marks of violence on his body. To this day we haven't the slightest idea how he died.

Two particularly distressing incidents happened in our last year that really have no place in a tale of

Africa; but both of which belong in a tale of the ups and downs of our strange and varied life.

The first one was an accident to myself. Every day we had been hearing elephants trumpeting across the lake, breaking down trees as they fed, and yet had not been able to get a good flashlight picture of the herd. So I decided to set up my apparatus across the lake. Usually I had two flash cartridges but this time, wanting a big picture, I used sixteen in nests of two each.

Now we were always very careful about stepping on the near side of the wire. The scent of animals is so powerful as to seem uncanny; for hours after you have set foot near a spot they will catch your scent. This is particularly true of the forest where there is no sun to destroy the smell. But careful as we were, this time some one blundered. I must have touched the spring, for there was a great roar and a light like that which greeted Saul on the road to Damascus, then all was blackness. And everywhere I went, blinded and groping, there was a singe of burning flesh in the air—my own. And, remembering the boy who had just died, I was more frightened than ever I had been when facing wild animals. After a while the boys who had been scared away by the great boom returned to my side, helped me to my feet and half led, half carried me, back to camp. Osa was out on the trail and there was not a living

JUST BEFORE THE BIG PARADE.

This is the still picture that Osa made while I was photographing the lions with the movie. We got a big thrill at this time. Before we started photographing the sun was under a cloud and the light bad, but soon the sun came out and we ground off four hundred feet of wonderful film as fourteen lions came in sight. Some of them sharpened their claws on trees like domestic cats.

THREE OUT OF FIFTEEN.

This picture is actually only a detail of the extraordinary scene we saw here. There were fifteen lions lying about in groups such as this when Carl Akeley and I came upon them. For two wonderful days we had the time of our lives. Then Carl got sick and Osa and I went on with the photographing work alone.

soul to give me any more skilled medical help than a drink of water, and this I could not swallow, so swollen were my lips. I really thought I could feel pieces of the flesh coming off from my body as I groaned on the blankets.

I began to picture the lockjaw which had attacked the boy. For this we had no serum in camp and were hundreds of miles from any surgeons. What worried me most was that the kerosene lamp the boys had lit gave out, for me, only the faintest and dimmest of glows. Outside of its little circle, which revealed no objects to me, the rest was utter darkness.

At last I heard voices and steps—then a very familiar voice—Osa's. She had heard the report of the eight times double charge of the flash cartridges, back in the woods, but at first thought it thunder. Then, seeing the stars through the trees, she had become worried and hastened with Ndundu back to camp.

There she had met the boys with scared faces, crying, "Bwana has had most awful accident." Perhaps she expected to see me dead; anyway, I must have been a horrifying sight to a white woman. They told me afterwards that I was black from head to foot and all blisters, the seared flesh showing even through the great burns in my clothes.

Poor Osa came running into my room, nearly in hysterics. The first thing she asked me was: "Can you see?" I said, "Yes." But she didn't believe me; she held up two fingers and asked me what she was doing. It was lucky she held them up so they were silhouetted against the light, as I could barely make out her hand, and that with one eye only.

She then proceeded to take off all the unguentine with which I had had the boys smear me. Assisted by the boys and John Wilshusen, who was with us, she worked over me until after midnight, using permanganate of potash. After they had cleaned my skin as much as possible of the powder, they put unguentine on again. By that time the burns were beginning to pain full force. There is no use going into details. In three days I could see a little out of my right eye, but not out of the left for two weeks more. It was only through Osa's nursing that I escaped the fate of the black who had died from lockjaw.

I recall the first day I could sit up in bed. I asked for a mirror. Goodness what a shock I got when I looked at myself! My nose had been knocked off to one side out of true. My left ear looked like a piece of cauliflower. I hadn't a hair left on my head; eyebrows and eyelashes gone. But worst of all my entire head down to my neck was black with the powder that had penetrated the skin. I had heard of miners being disfigured for life this way; and decided that the same thing had become my fate. But after a few weeks the skin came off, the black with it, and now I have practically no marks left.

The other misfortune to which I refer was the death of our little Kalowatt, the ape whom we loved like a child. It happened when we went down to Nairobi to meet the Eastman-Pomeroy party.

No one ever had a nicer pet than this little ape, which was just a ball of fluff, little larger than a man's fist. She was more intelligent than any other animal I have ever seen. She was affectionate, and loved everybody that knew her. She had travelled all over the world with us and was the only animal that I have seen that could laugh. Once I had been offered two thousand dollars for her; but I would not have taken two million.

I was in the Norfolk Hotel at Nairobi and had just gone out into the lobby to talk with Philip Percival who was also waiting the Eastman party to act as big game hunter. While sitting there I suddenly saw Osa running towards me.

"Kalowatt has got out of our room and is on the roof!" she exclaimed.

Now Kalowatt as a rule would obey our commands. But I suppose she had been cramped up in our room so long that she welcomed the opportunity to stretch her legs.

As I was busy, I didn't go out, but let Osa see what she could do to overtake the little rascal. Kalowatt ran across the roof, jumped into the trees in front of the hotel and played about with a large audience of natives looking on. She always loved a crowd before which she could show off. From where I sat I watched her for a while and thought there was no danger of her running away. Finally she left the trees, jumped on the roof again and ran across the building to the back of the hotel out of my sight, Osa following.

In a few minutes Osa came dashing back. "My God!" she cried. "I have just seen Kalowatt electrocuted. She jumped on two live wires on the side of the hotel. I saw a puff of smoke. Then she hung limp to the wires." At this Osa fainted. I left her with Percival.

I rushed out and saw Kalowatt hanging there, still gripped to the wires about fifteen feet above the alley. A large crowd of gaping natives stood around, some of them grinning. I simply went crazy when I saw this, and crazier than ever when one of the blacks broke out laughing. Losing all semblance of control, I waded into the mob and knocked the negroes right and left. While I was doing this a doctor who was staying at the hotel came out to see what was wrong. I knocked him down too. The cook came out carrying a bucketful of water; I knocked him down.

I went back to the hotel. Osa had been carried

to our rooms. I found her sobbing her heart out on the bed. I walked up and down the room unable to believe it was true that we had lost our little companion.

Meanwhile Percival had telephoned the electric light company to have the power turned off. A boy climbed the telegraph pole and got the little dead body down. I went out and wrapped what was left of Kalowatt in a blanket and brought her into our room and placed her in the little cage that we had always carried her in. This cage was very small. I had spent a lot of money getting a bigger cage made, but Kalowatt never liked anything except this little one.

There followed a night of grief for Osa and me. Near midnight we couldn't stand it any longer. We went out and got one of our motor cars and drove way out on the Athi plains, got out and walked up and down until daylight. At dawn we went back to the hotel, took Kalowatt's cleanest blankets which had just been washed, and wrapped her up in them. Then I went out and bought a tin rubber-lined officer's dress case. We put the body in this and placed it on the back seat of our motor. It was a peculiar fact that the African boys who had been with me did not show up that morning. Despite the fact that the blacks are supposed to be almost without feeling, they didn't want to come up and see the dead body of Kalowatt, whom they had known for so long and so happily. I think they loved her almost as much as we did.

We mustered two or three Nairobi boys and drove ten miles out into the country to a forest reserve that was not likely to be touched by man for many years. We selected a site under a large tree, and the boys dug a six-foot grave. We placed Kalowatt in it, and beside her the cage that had been her home.

We now went back to Lake Paradise for our last visit. There were loose ends to tie and a last few pictures to make. Though we had been in Africa only three years and ten months, we found it was not necessary to stay the extra year we had planned for in the beginning. Our luck with the lions and elephants had been such that we all felt reasonaby satisfied with the film we had got. So we decided to return to America with what we had.

When we were all packed we decided to leave several boys at Lake Paradise to look after the place in order that we might come back to it some time in the following year or so. I sent word out to the caravans that passed on the plains telling the Samali that on a certain day we would hold a sale of our goods that we did not need to take home with us. When the natives turned up they were the most wild-looking gang of cutthroats that I have ever seen. We had arranged in piles our cooking utensils, buckets, boxes, riffraff of tools, old knives that had accumulated and various other kinds of material. It was all auctioned off with a total return of over six hundred shillings for which cash was paid.

My assistant, John Wilshusen, helped us get away some days later. I'd like to say here that John was one of the most satisfactory safari companions I've ever had. He was a wonderful mechanic and could fix anything from a watch to a threshing machine. He was an old flying man, having been to South America with the Hamilton Rice expedition. He was a great lad to speed; he figured he was standing still if he was making less than sixty miles an hour on a fair road. He even surprised George Blowers, who had hitherto been the speed king of Nairobi. When he saw John whisking around in our fine Willys-Knights he told me I'd better get the lad out on the Athi Plains as life was no longer safe in Nairobi.

We set out a week behind the wagons we had sent ahead with some of our stuff. We crossed the Kaisoot Desert as fast as the cars would travel. Certainly if any cars ever had a test, ours did, between rocks and mud and grades.

In Meru we got word of Carl Akeley's death. This was a big shock because Carl spoke our language and was one of the finest men that ever lived. His versatility had always astonished me. He was a sculptor, inventor of the famous Akeley camera, a splendid photographer, and the father of a new system of taxidermy that is now being used throughout the world.

At Nairobi we set out to find ourselves a house that could be our home in the future. We had definitely decided to make Africa our permanent residence henceforth, and visit America only as occasion demanded. It was primarily through the generosity of Mr. Daniel Pomeroy of New York that this dream of ours could come true. As our object from now on through the rest of our lives is to make a true pictorial history of the different kinds of African wild animals, and since Nairobi is the logical center to work from, we felt that we have chosen the proper location for our home.

For the first time in our married life Osa and I now have a home that is really our own. Up to this time Lake Paradise had been our refuge and it had given us many happy years. But of it Osa used to say, laughingly, that when I married her I promised her a palace, and the nearest she ever got to it was a mudhouse.

We have four acres of ground, a fine orchard of fruit trees, pears, apples, peaches, plums, all growing beside oranges, mandarins, lemons, limes, and other kinds of tropical and sub-tropical fruits. One of the first things Osa did was to plant a fine strawberry bed.

STEALING A LITTLE THUNDER FROM A LUMBWA VICTORY.

This is probably the last picture Carl Akeley had taken before he died. He is at the left, holding the cigarette—then follow myself, then the two best white hunters in Africa—Pat Ayre and Philip Percival.

THE SONG OF TRIUMPH.

Lumbwa spearmen doing a chanting ceremony around a lion's body which has just been speared. These people are not very demonstrative. After every lion speared, they do a short chant around the carcase, and then slowly march away in search of another lion.

On the land we erected a stone walled laboratory with tiled roof.   I installed the best filters and tanks I could buy.   I lined the whole place with tile so that I could have my boys take the hose and scrub the inside as well as out.   The main house has eight rooms, running hot and cold water in several of them; large tiled bathroom; a fine kitchen with electric light and ice machine equipment, bringing it all up to date.

The place is situated four miles outside of Nairobi. To the south we can see Mt. Kilimanjaro with its snow-covered peak springing up from the level plains. To the north Mt. Kenya stands sentinel over the hunting preserve we know so well. Wild animals come into our garden every night. The house stands well back from the road with an attractive drive curving up to it through special landscape gardening put in by an English expert. As we have room for seven cars we can take care of a moderate sized expedition coming out from America.

We remained in Nairobi for about ten days getting settled and tying up loose ends after our years of dashing about the country. One pleasant little jaunt came when we took a trip up to the Lumbwa country, about one hundred seventy miles up the railway toward Lake Victoria Nyanza. We had heard of some very primitive natives that I had wanted to see, and I was anxious to have a look around in that direction for my next spell of African work.

We chartered a little four-wheel two compartment coach and travelled direct to the Lumbwa station, a small isolated outpost. There we remained for two weeks photographing this strange group of humans and learning something about their native habits. We had first become interested in them when we had seen their wonderful lion spearing down in Tanganyika, which I have already described.

We journeyed back to Nairobi again in our "private car." I shall never forget the ride. In small towns in our own middle west I have seen antique railway cars that somewhat resembled this one. It was impossible for us to sleep in it, as its vertical motion was alone almost as great as that of an ocean liner in a storm.

We remained in Nairobi this time about three weeks longer. Somehow the closer we got to the end the harder it was to tear ourselves away. Thus has it always been on our journeys to the ends of the earth. I remember Dana speaking of the same thing at the finish of his *Two Years Before the Mast*. He relates how he got back to Boston after that hard voyage and found himself moved to stay aboard instead of dashing home to luxury.

We went down to Mombasa on the train and put up for a day or two waiting for the boat that was to take us to northern latitudes again. We were pleased to find that our ship was to be the *Bernardin*

Saint Pierre, a new fifteen thousand ton steamer of the Messageri Maritime Line. She took sixteen days en route to Marseilles, proving one of the most comfortable and luxurious vessels on which I have ever travelled.

Thence our trail led to Paris where Osa spent the few remaining dollars in our bank account on Paris gowns. As she had not had anything pretty for many a moon she naturally revelled in the fineries of that wonderful city. She even persuaded me to join her on some of her shopping tours.

After Osa's dressmakers and milliners had been settled I just barely had enough cash left to buy two tickets on the *Leviathan* bound home. We reached New York on May 16, 1927. For six months we have endured the horrors of traffic, telephones, telegraphs, carbon dioxide, banquets, week-end parties, boiled shirts, poisonous cocktails, suburban trains and a thousand other tormenting details of civilization.

We have survived, thanks I think, to the health and strength we had gained during our long sojourn in Africa. But when December approached we secretly decided to give each other what seemed at the time the nicest Christmas presents in the world. These presents didn't take up much room; in fact the two of them were small enough to slip into my waistcoat pocket. When Osa saw them she threw

her arms around my neck and we laughed and cried
for joy.

The Christmas present we chose for one another
was a ticket apiece back to Africa.

THE END